I0416616

Dear parents, We want to express our sincere gratitude for providing your child with the wonderful opportunity to explore a colorful world full of learning through this animal coloring book. By investing in this activity, you are not only stimulating your children's creativity and fine motor coordination, but also promoting precious moments of connection and learning with them. Thank you for cultivating a love of art and discovery from an early age. May these pages be filled with joy, imagination and special memories between you and your children.

Marcelo Pedro
2024

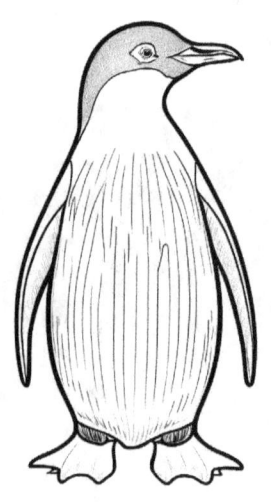

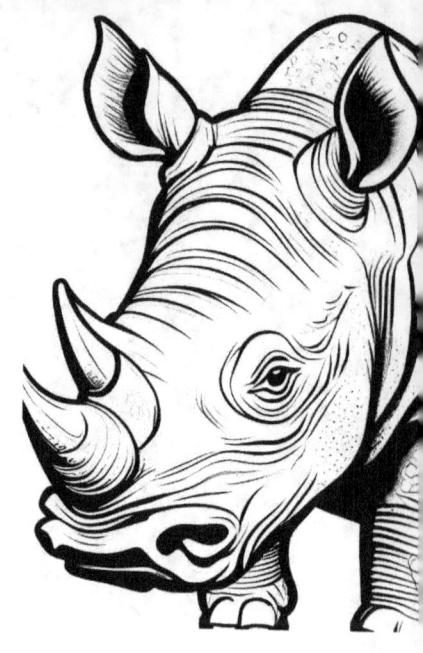

This Book Belongs to:

○─────────────────────────────────────○

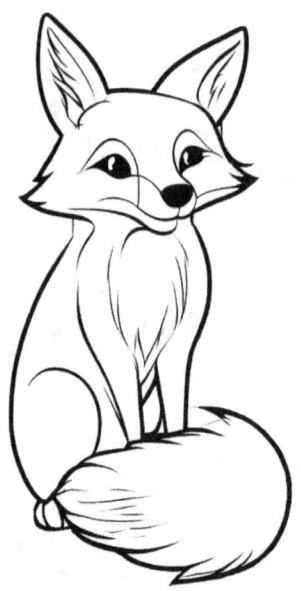

M.P.P.©
all rights reserved

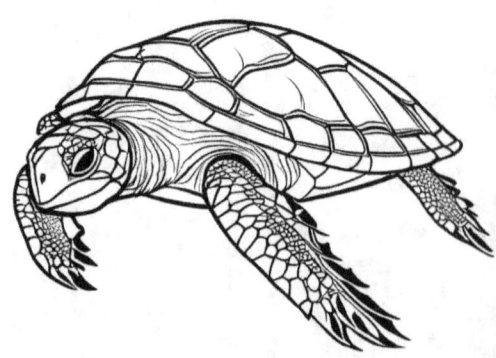

ALL RIGHTS RESERVED©
2024

No part of this publication may be reproduced, distributed or transmitted in any form or by any means, including photocopying, recording, or other electronic or mechanical methods, without the prior written permission of the publisher, except brief quotations embodied in critical reviews and other uses not specific commercials. Any unauthorized replication of this work is prohibited.

M.P.P.©
Marcelo Pedro Publications

Test Color Page

CAT

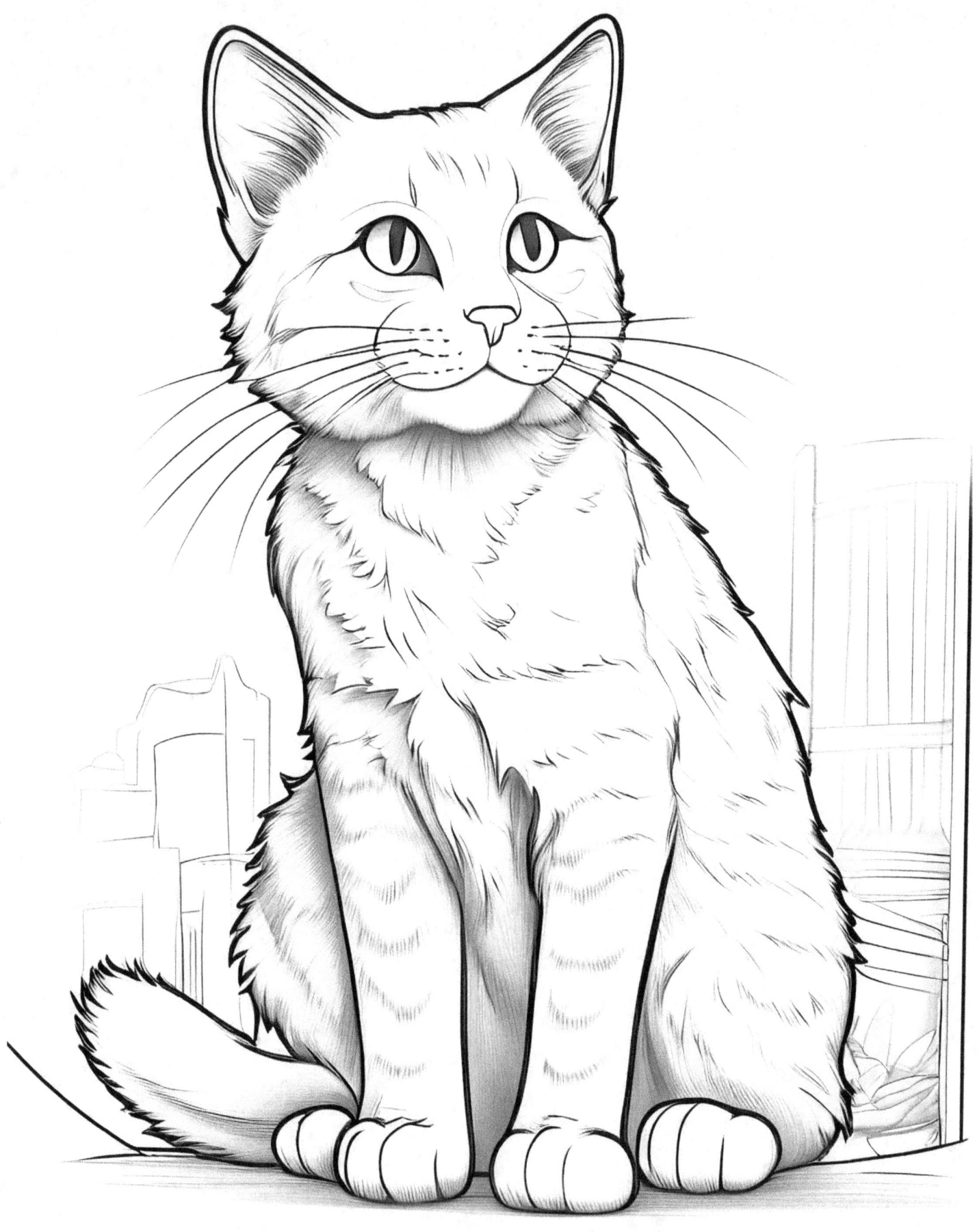

Horse

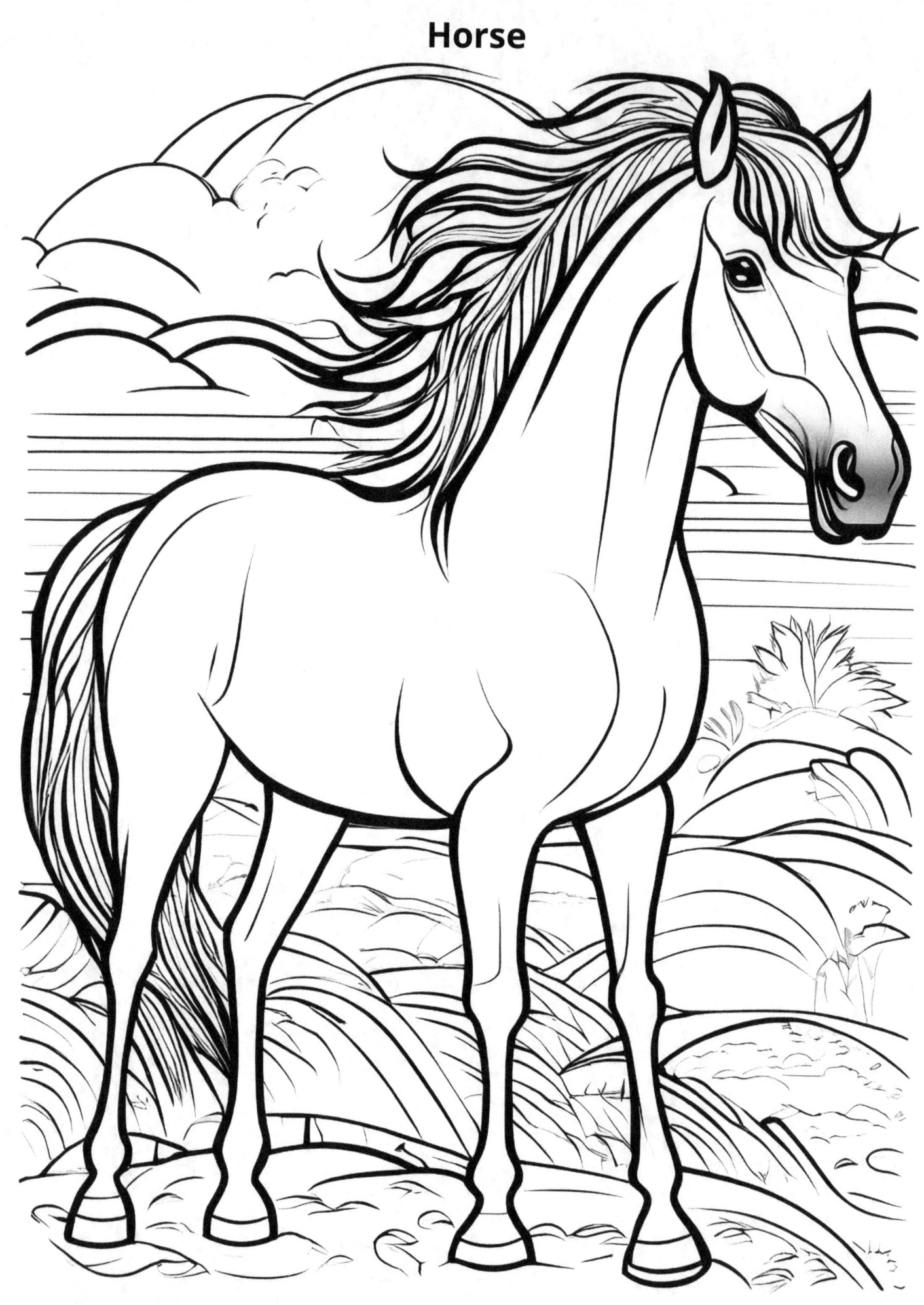

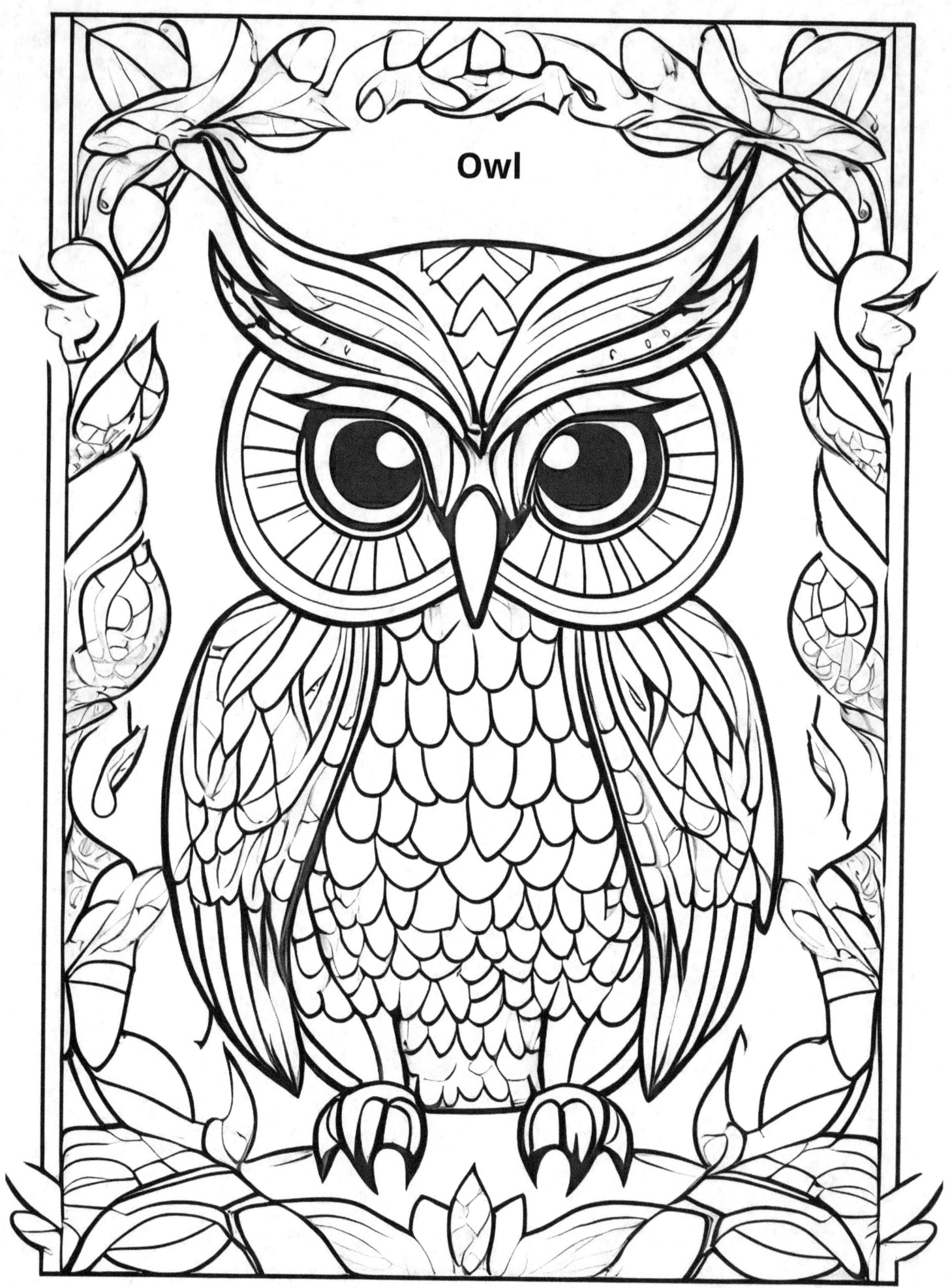

Owl

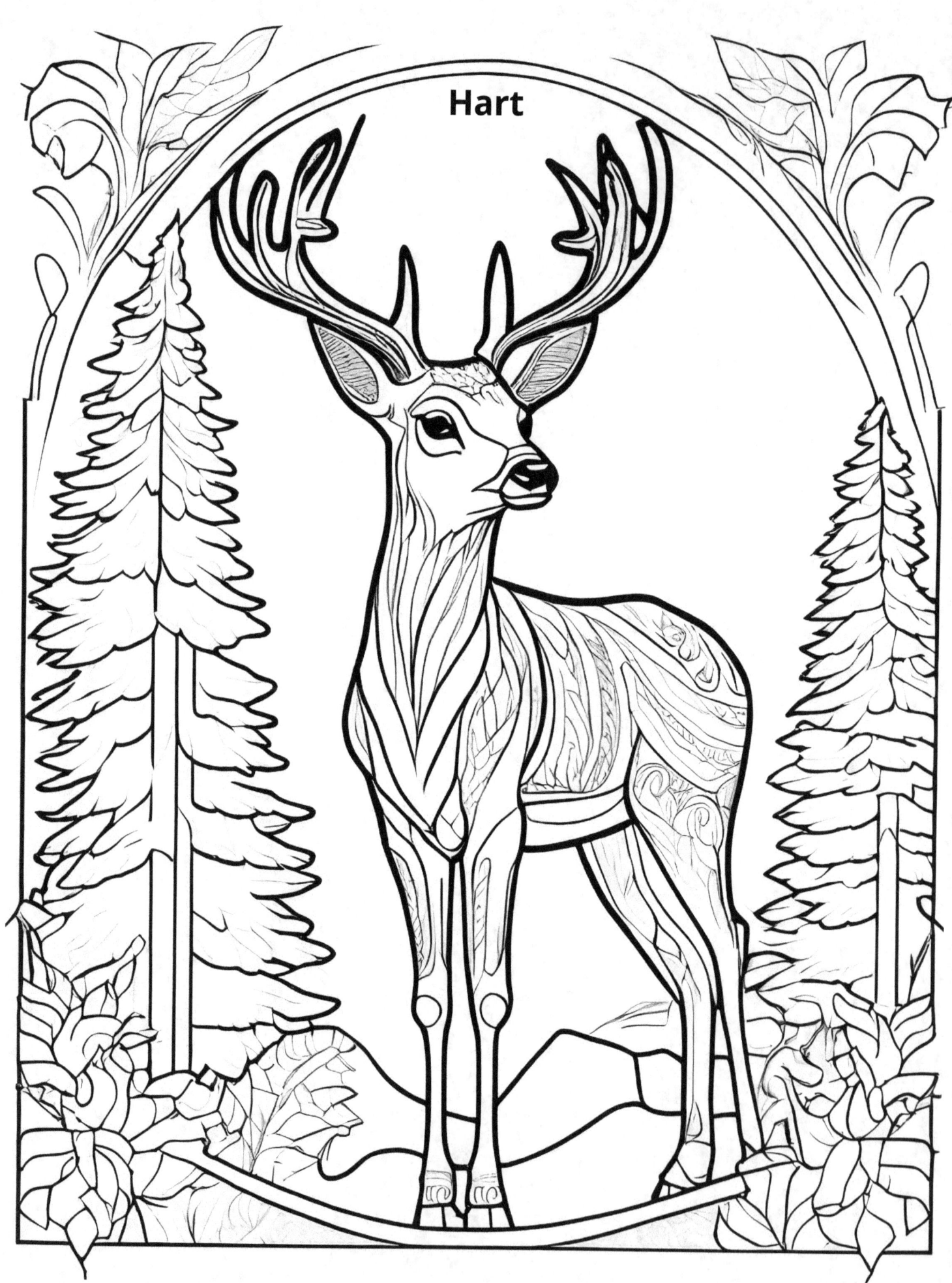

Hart

Capybara

Seahorse

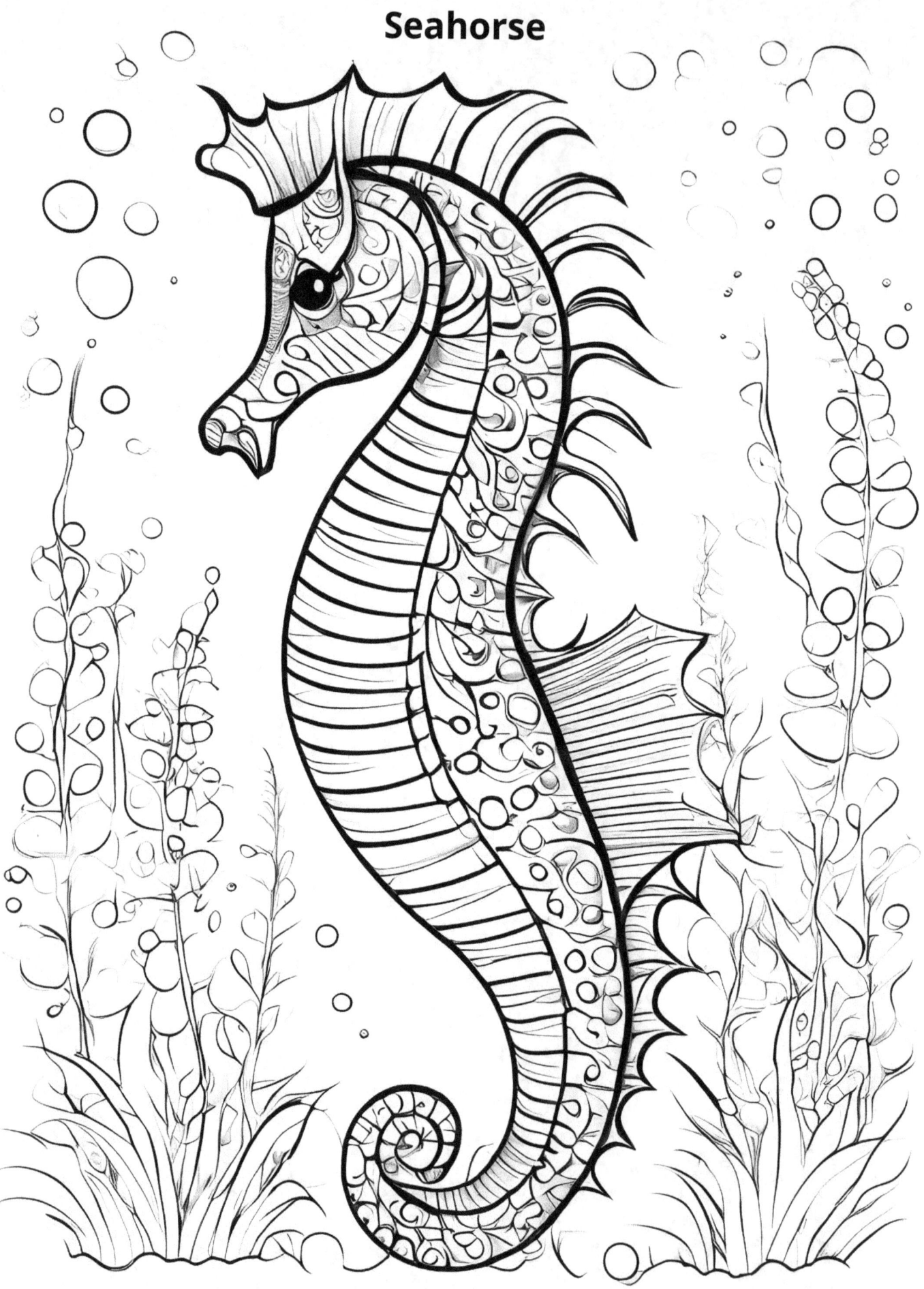

Sloth

Kangaroo

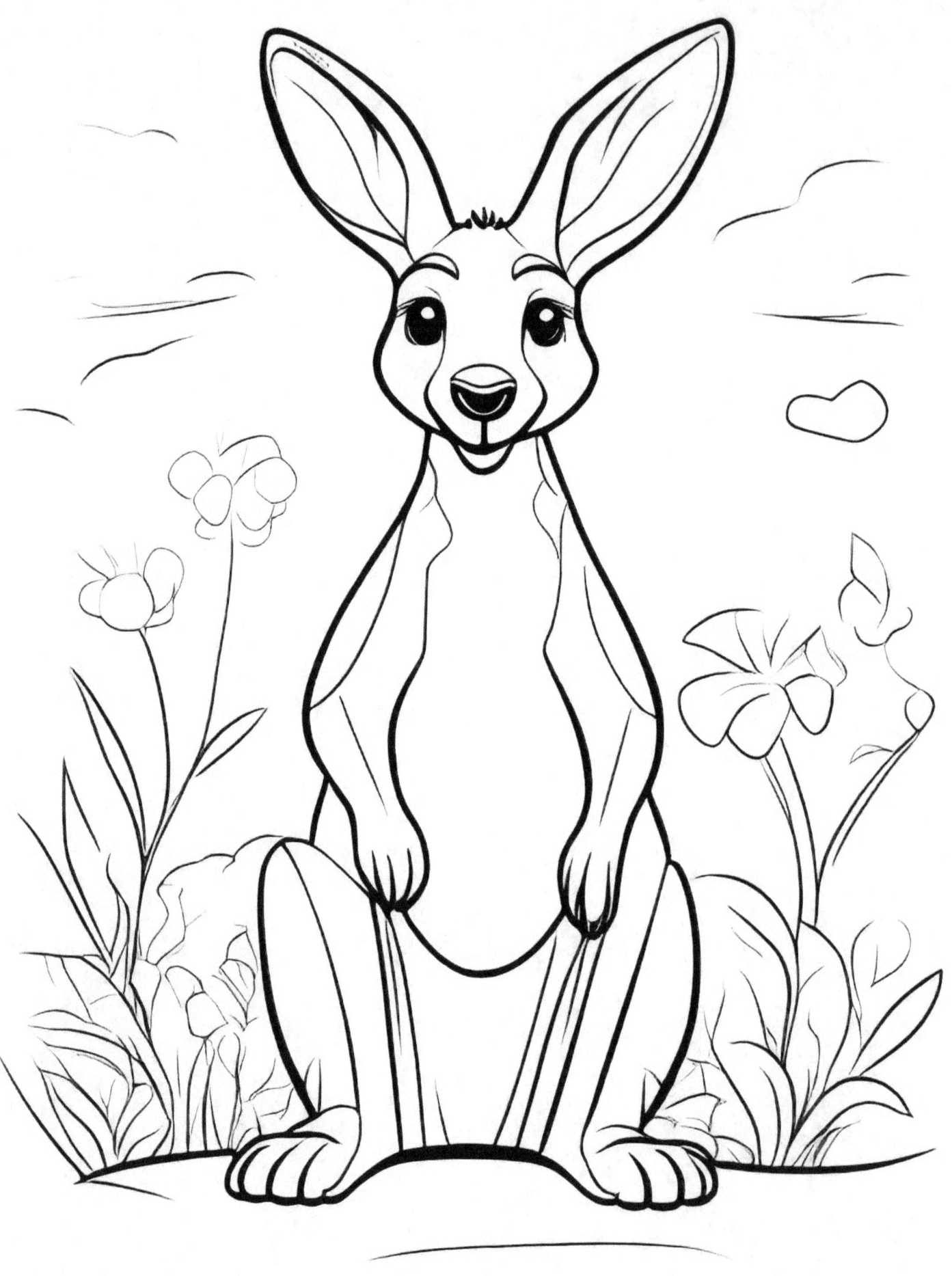

Hummingbird

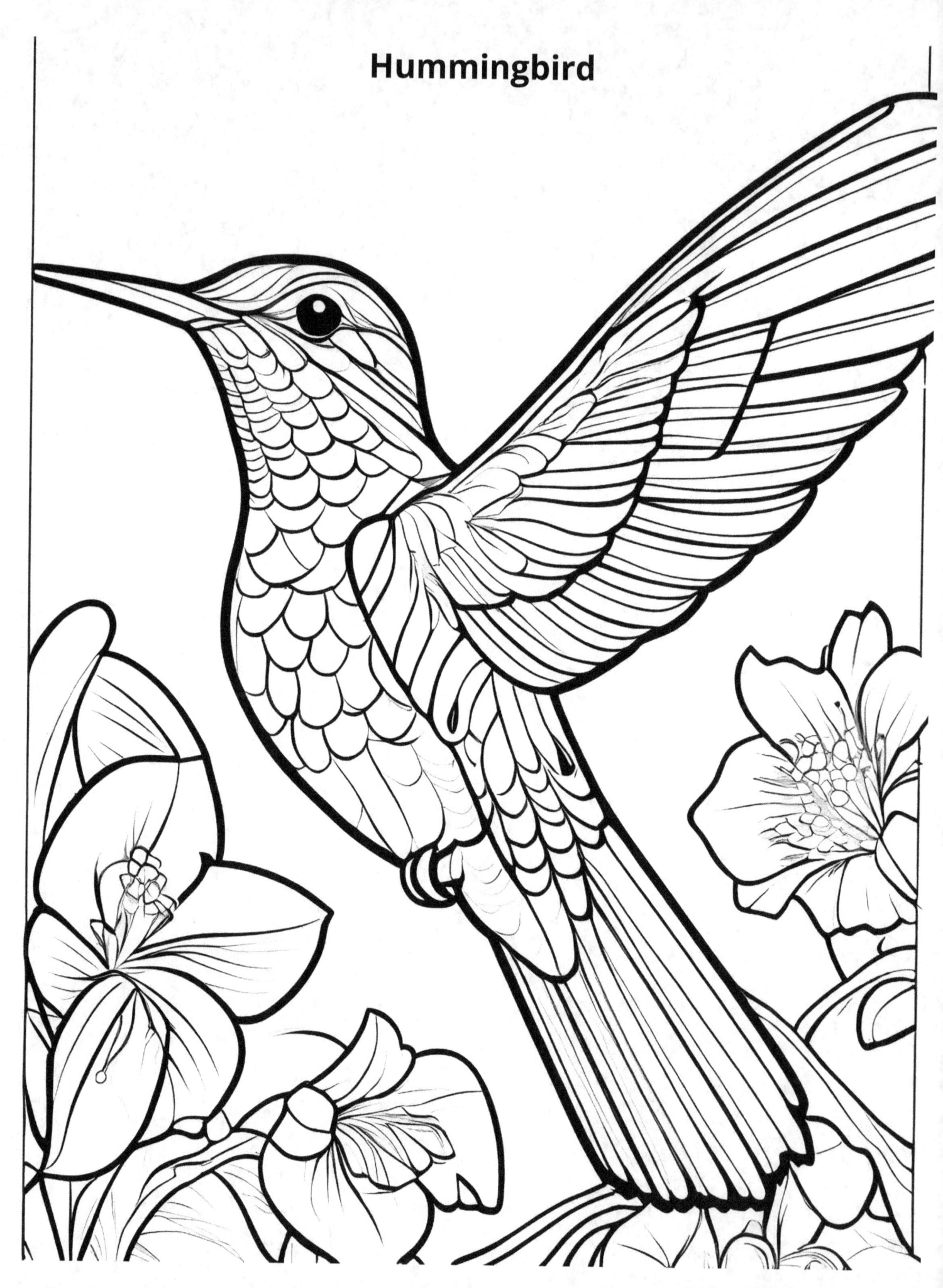

Crab

Hawk

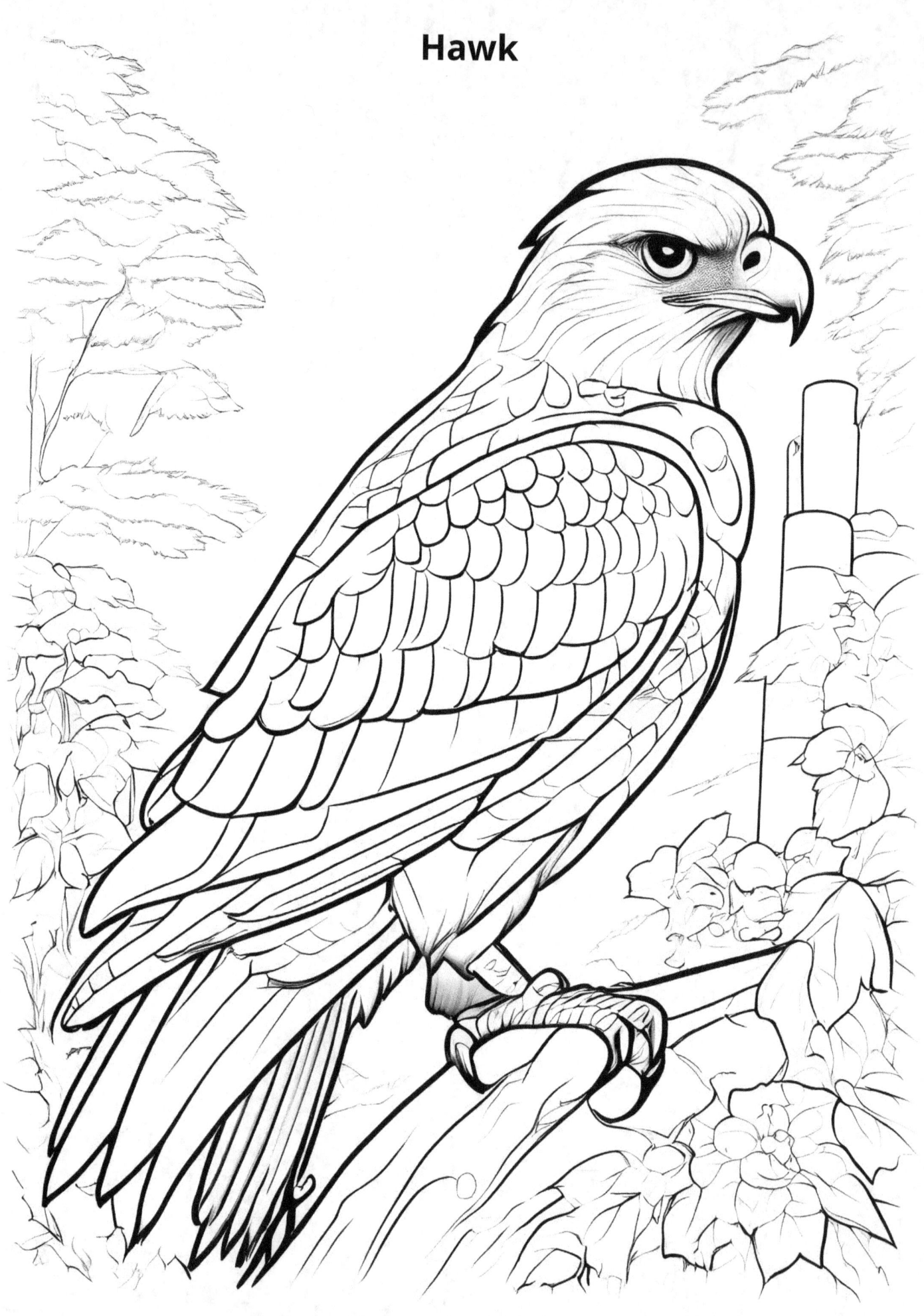

Hen

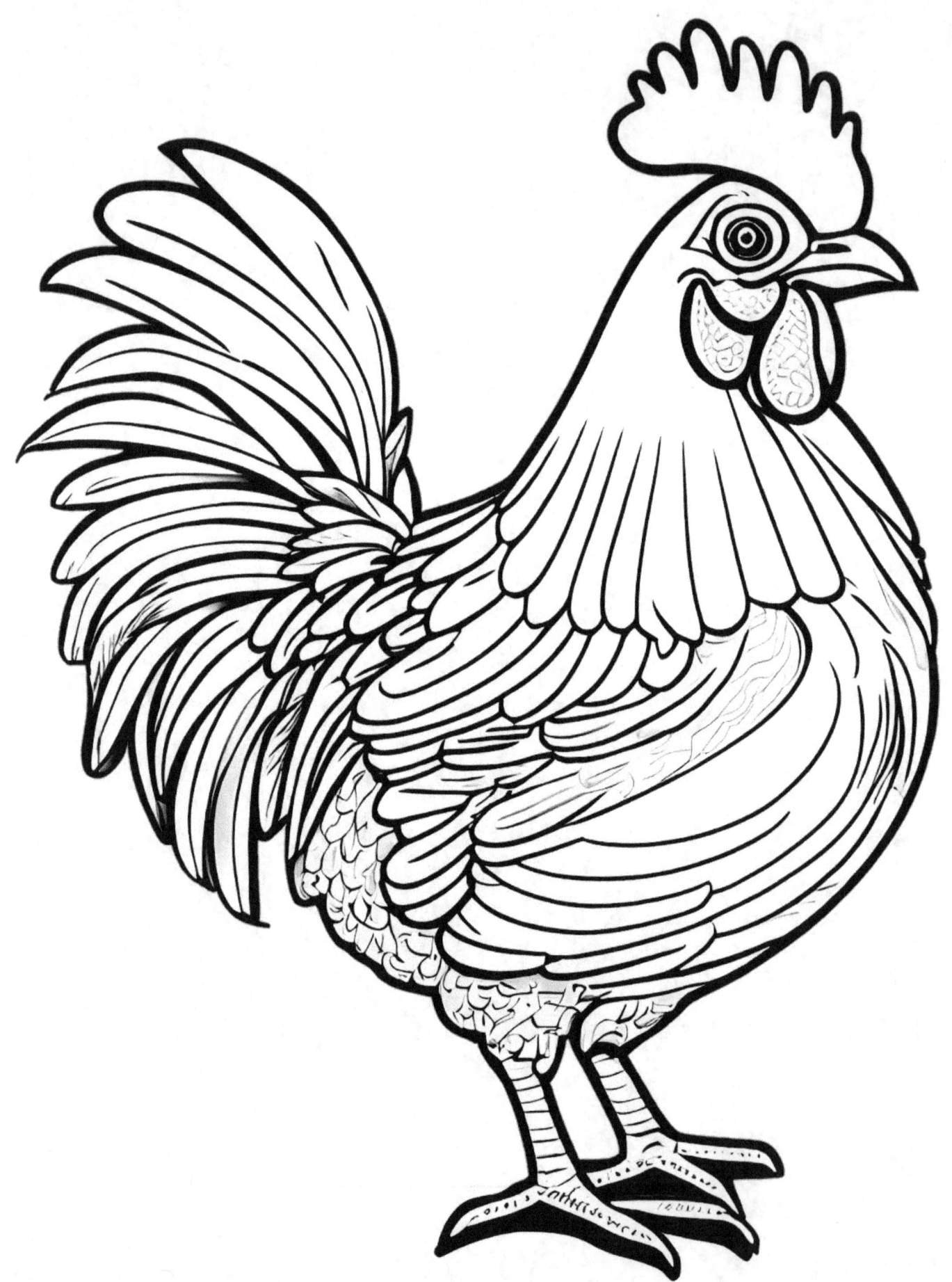

Starfish

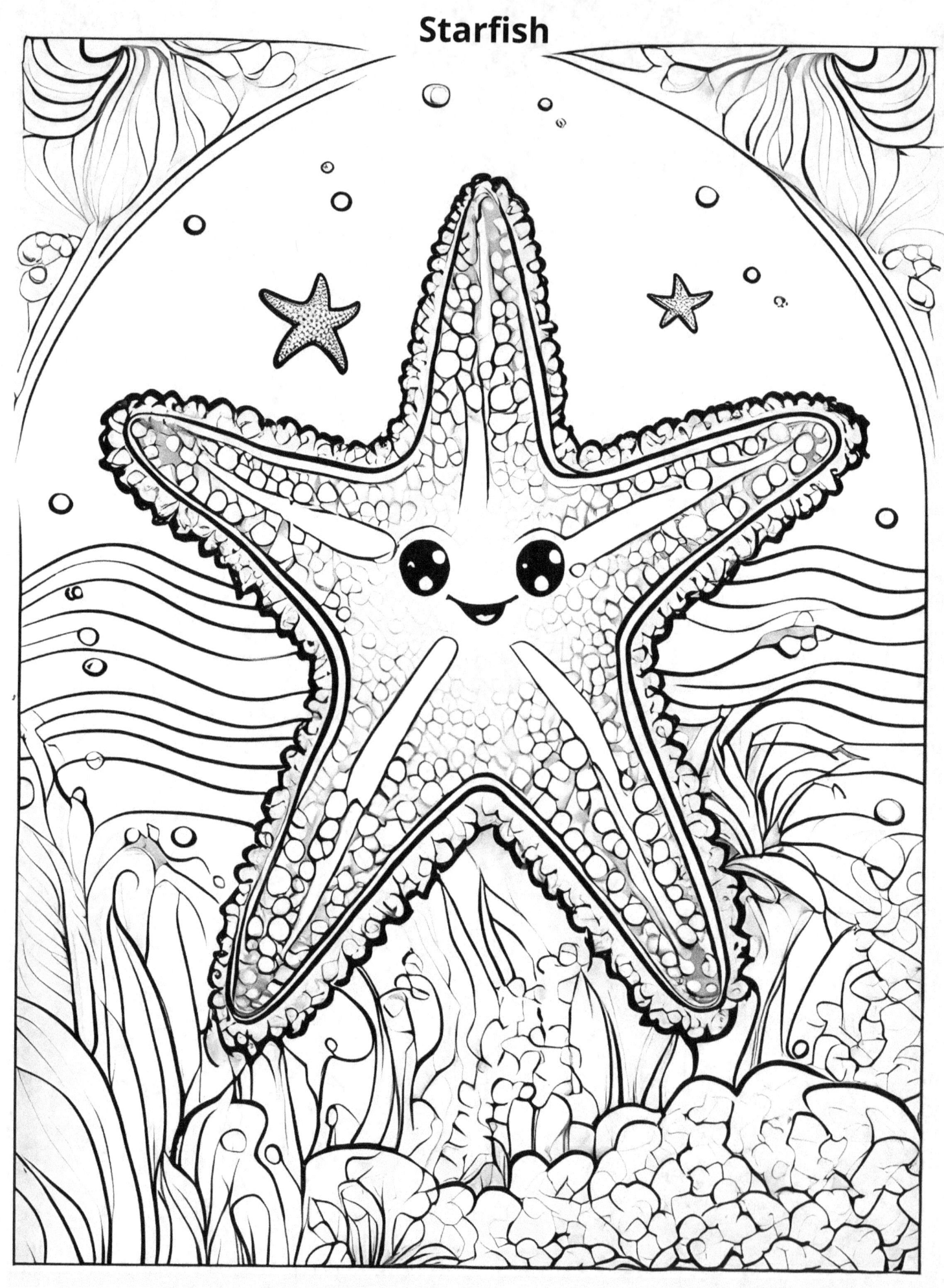

Rabbit

Flamingo

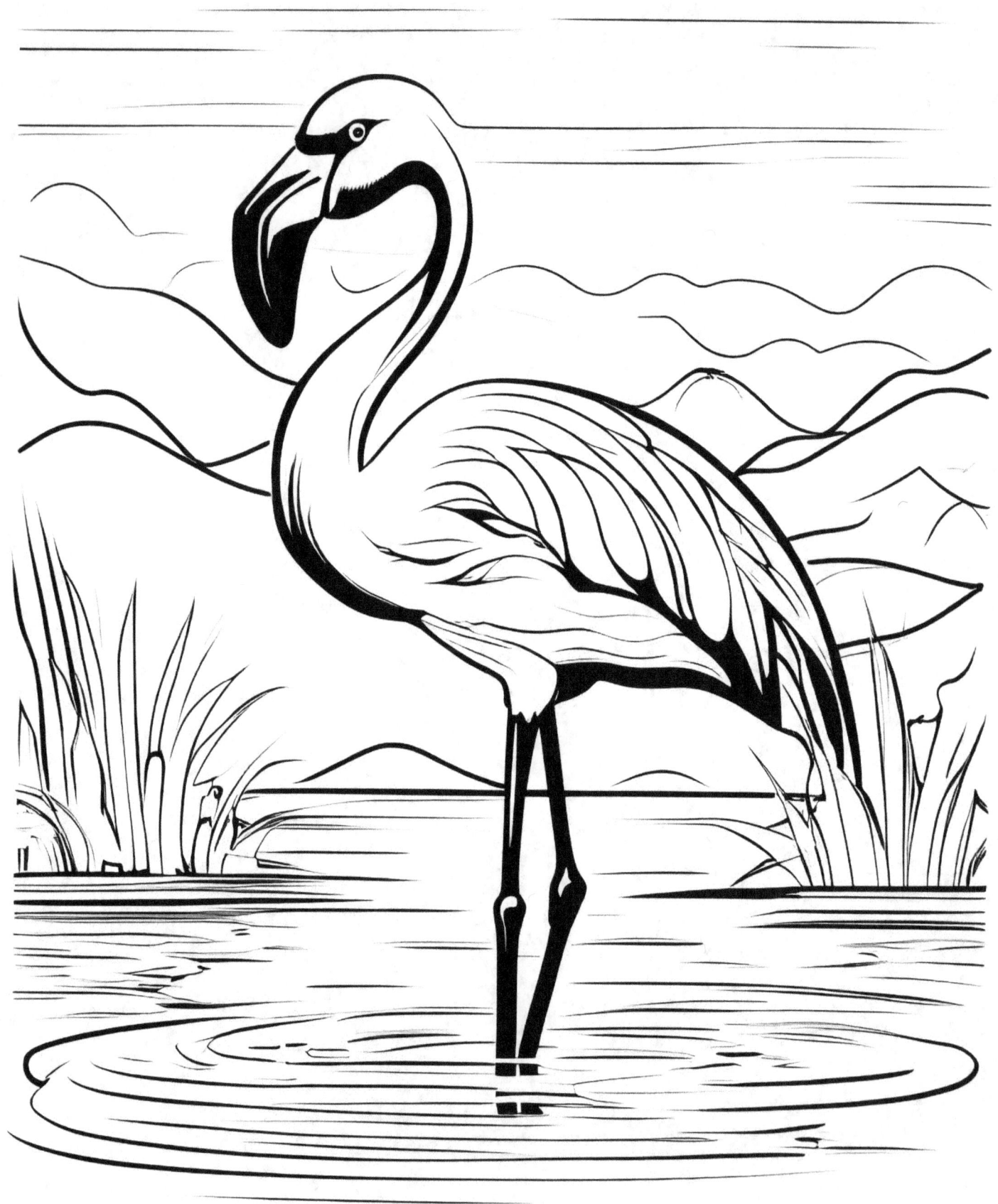

Dolphin

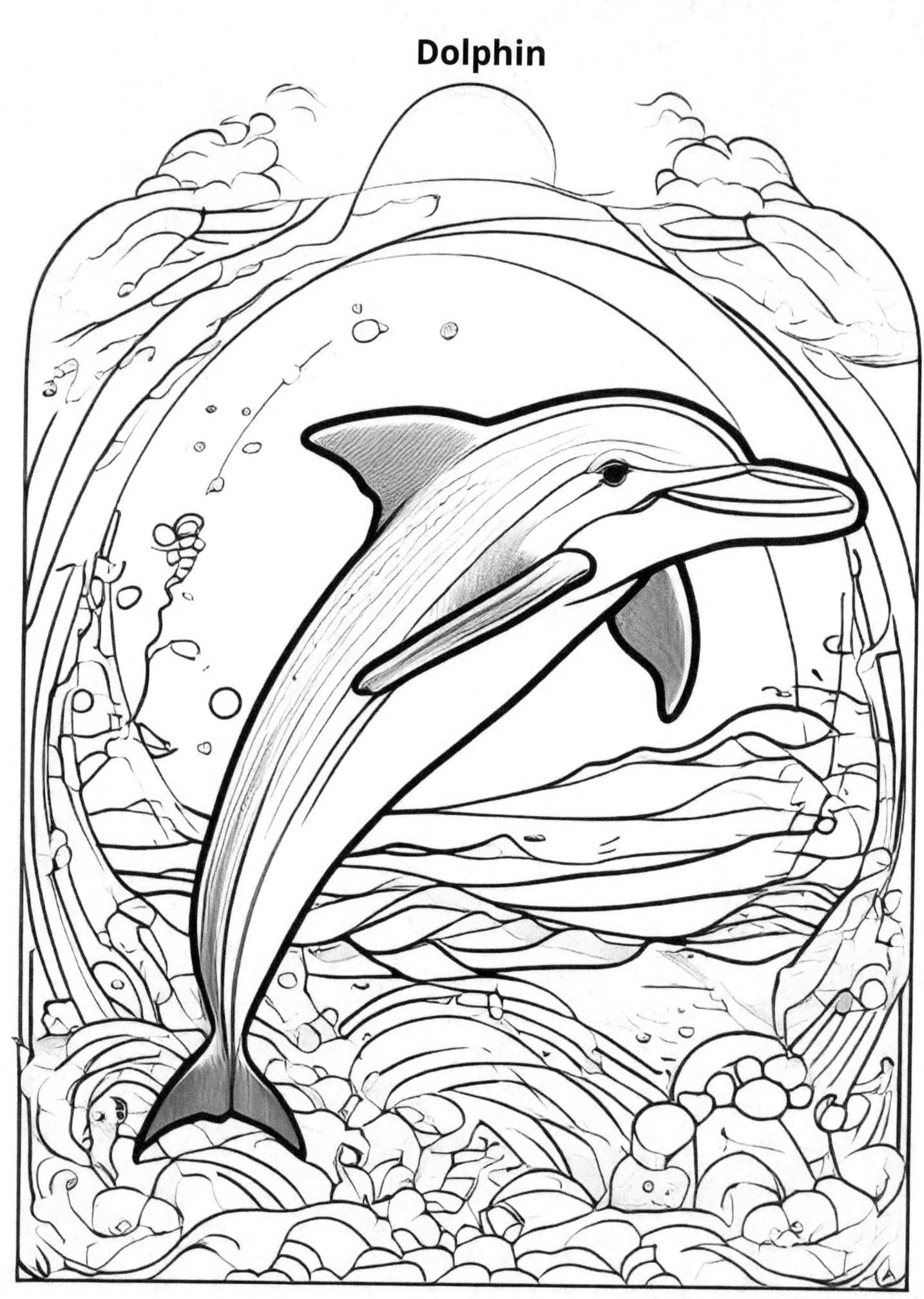

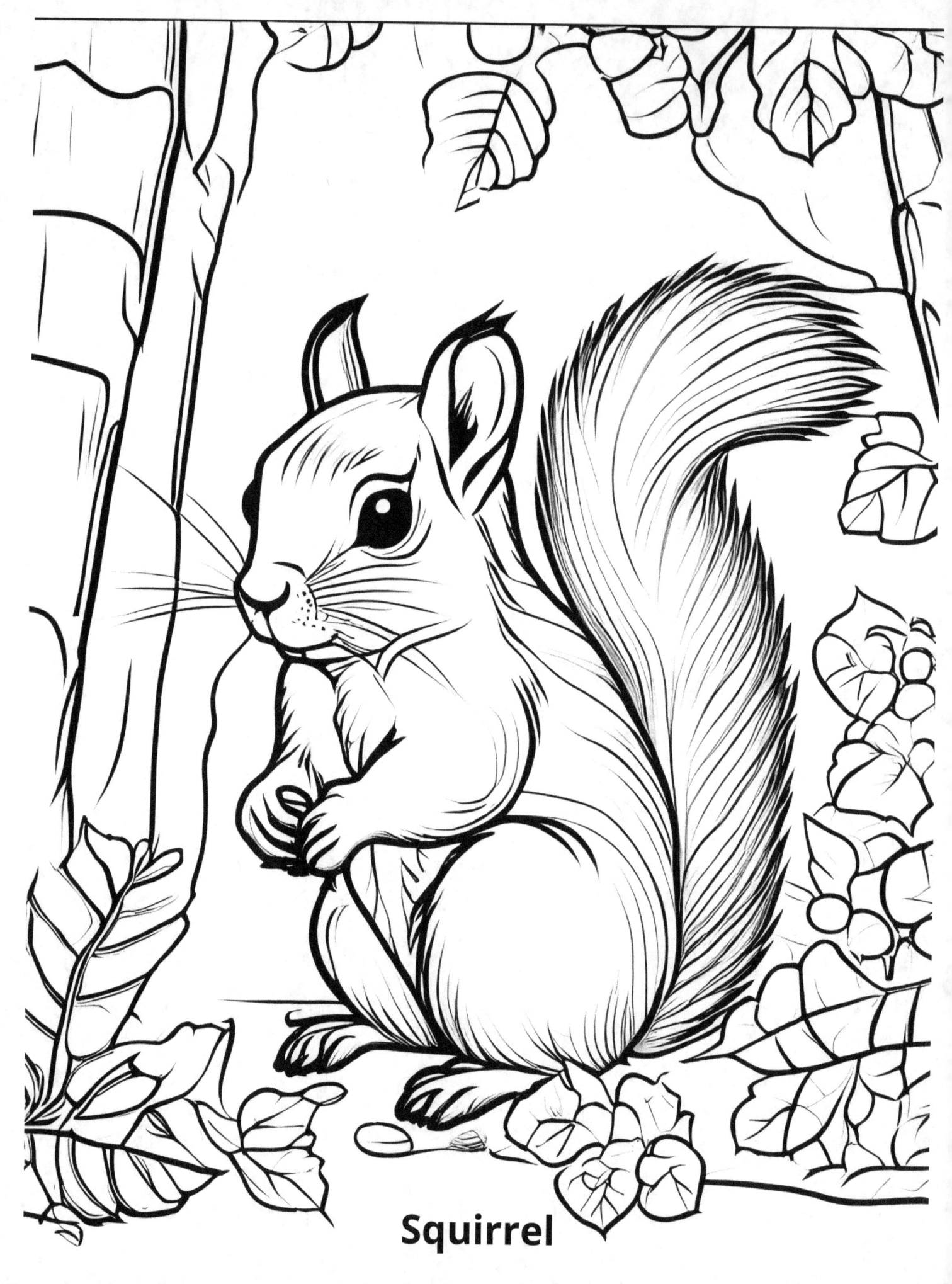

Squirrel

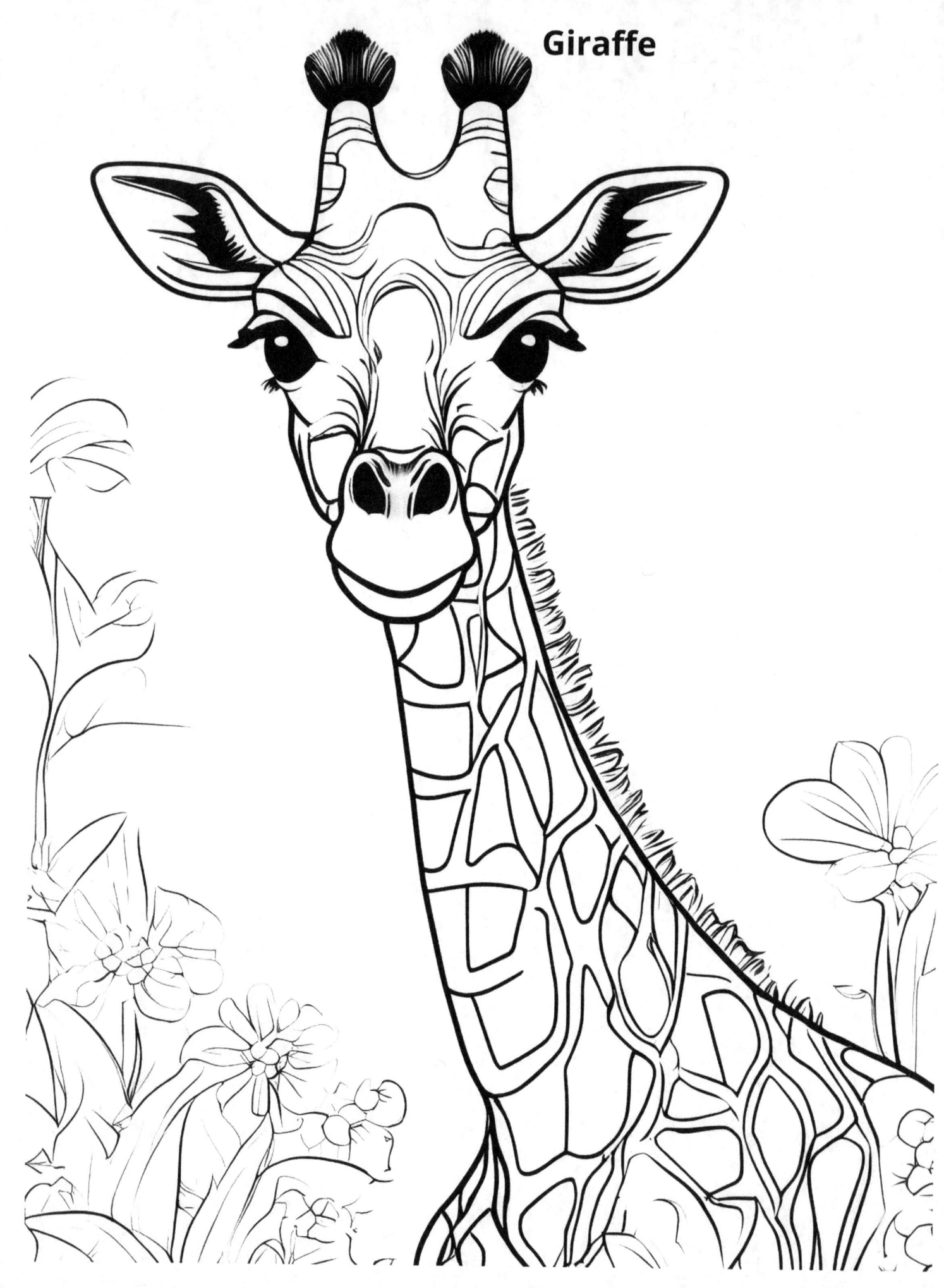

Giraffe

Elephant

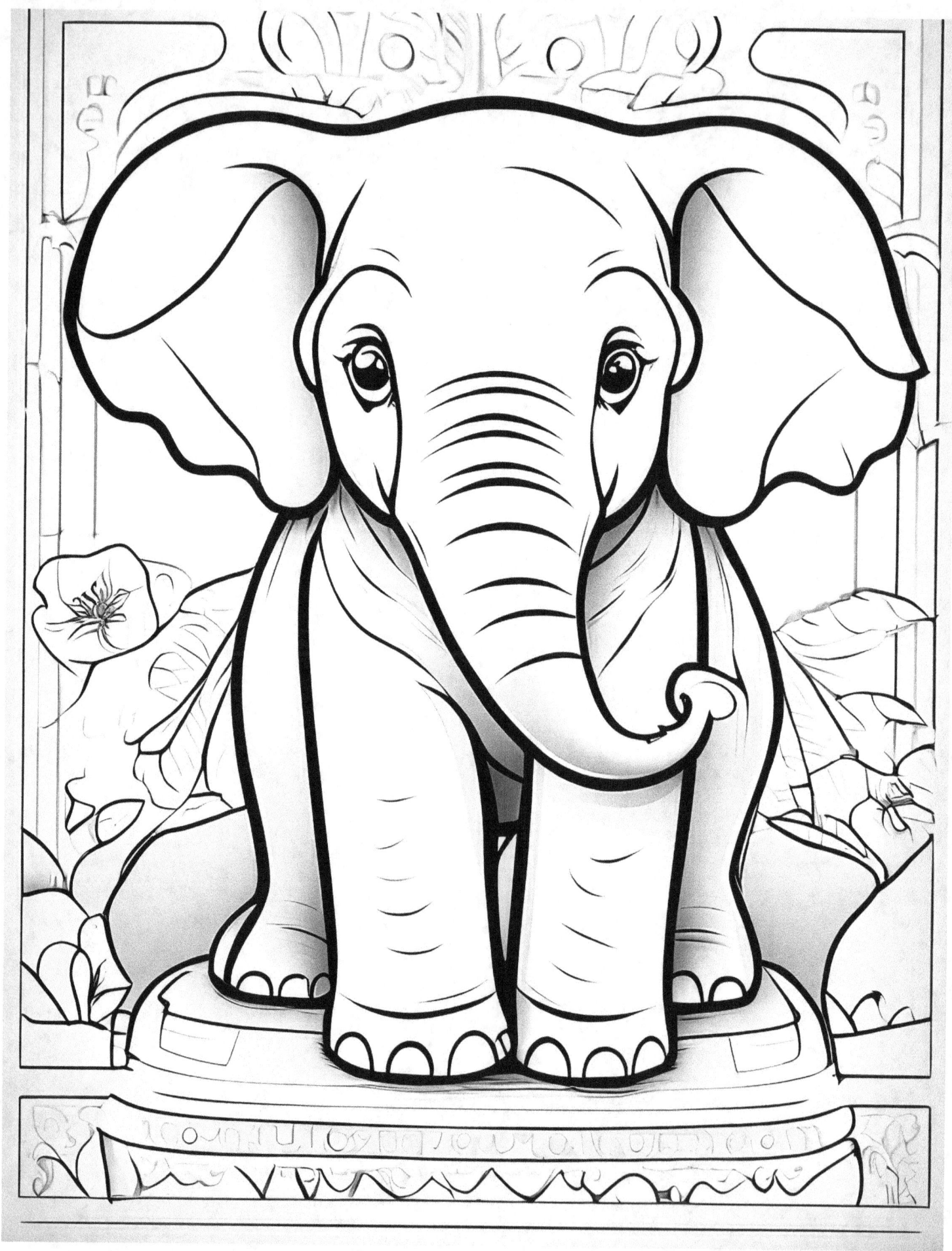

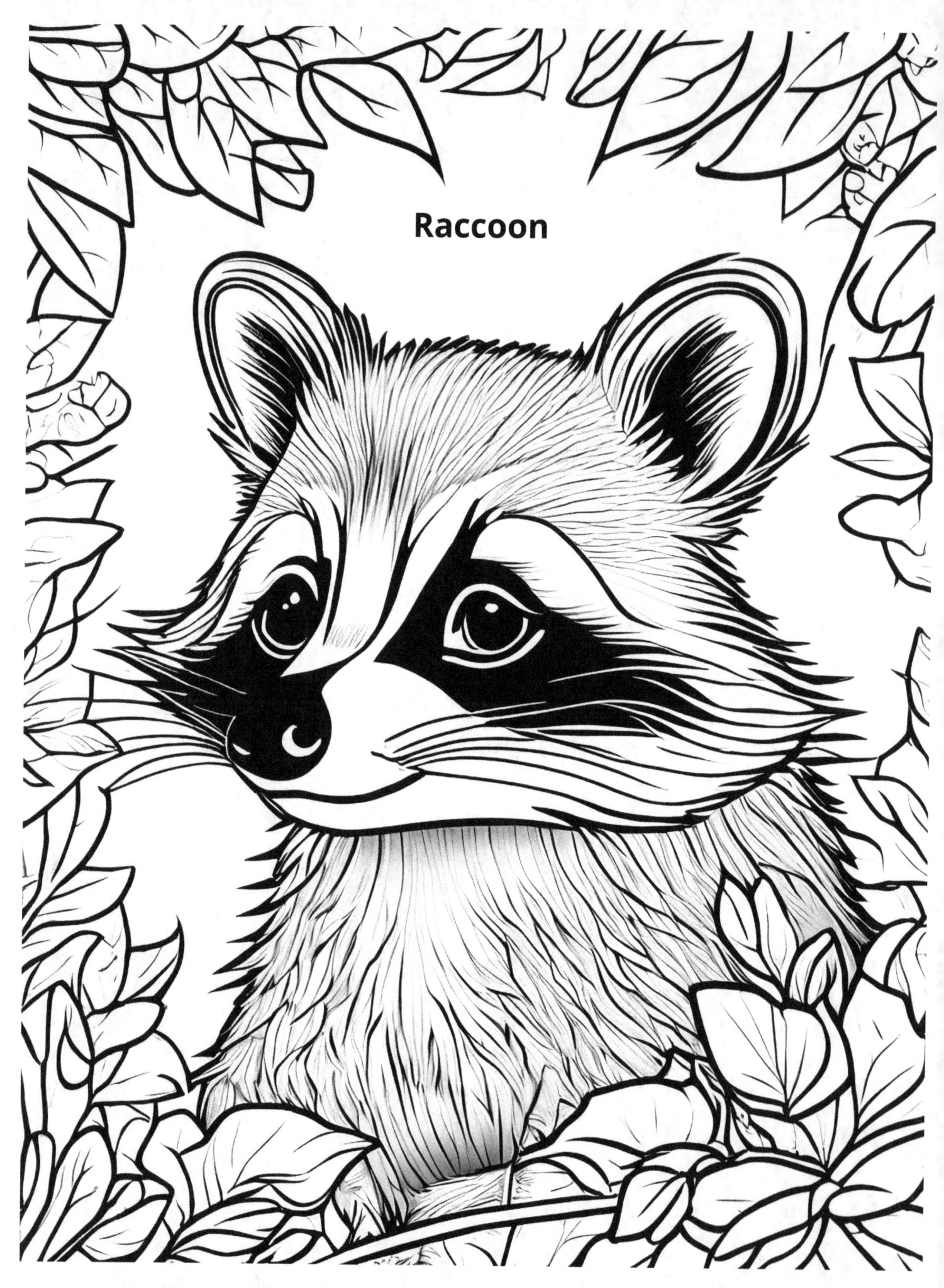

Raccoon

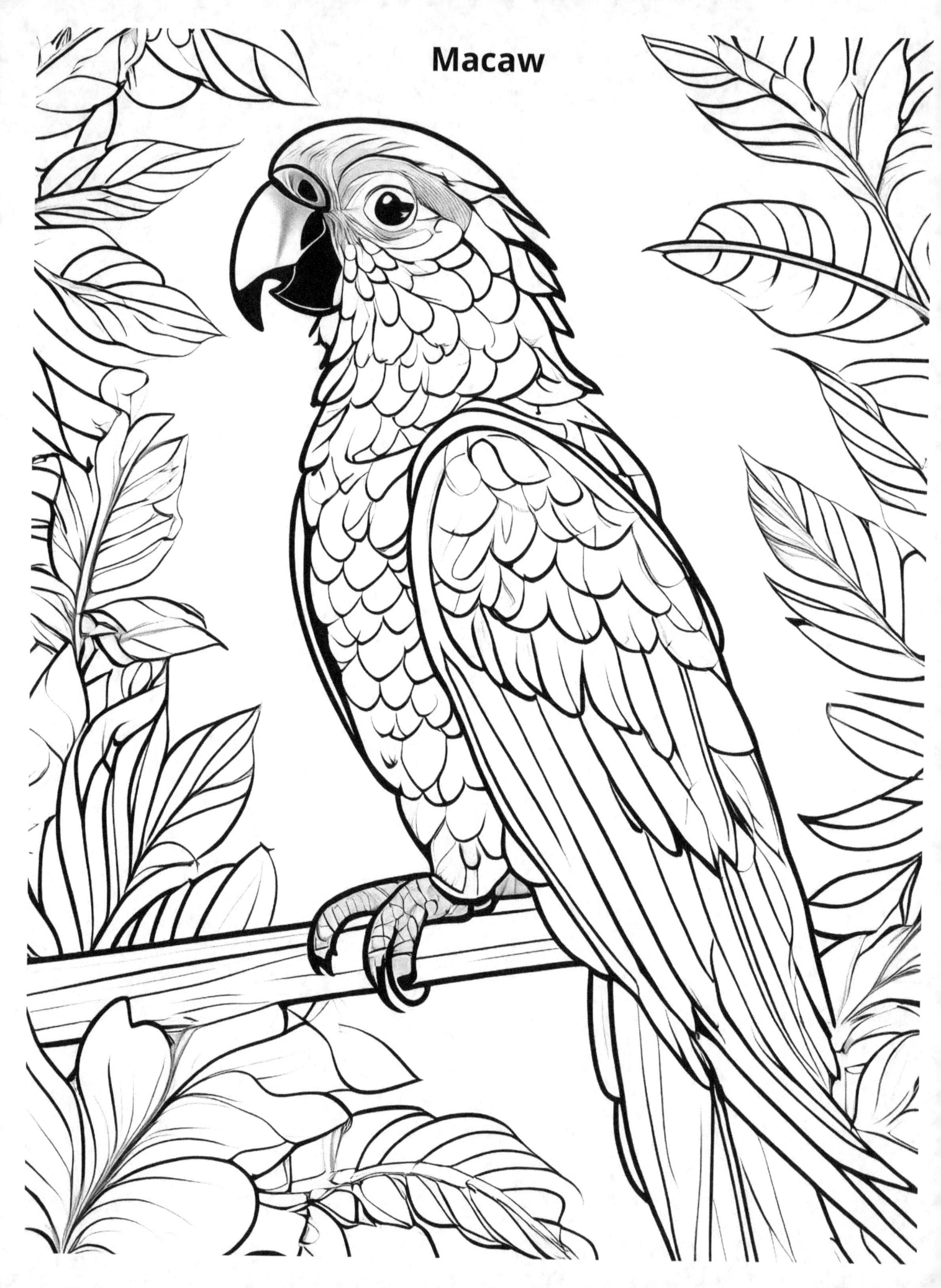

Macaw

Hipoppotamus

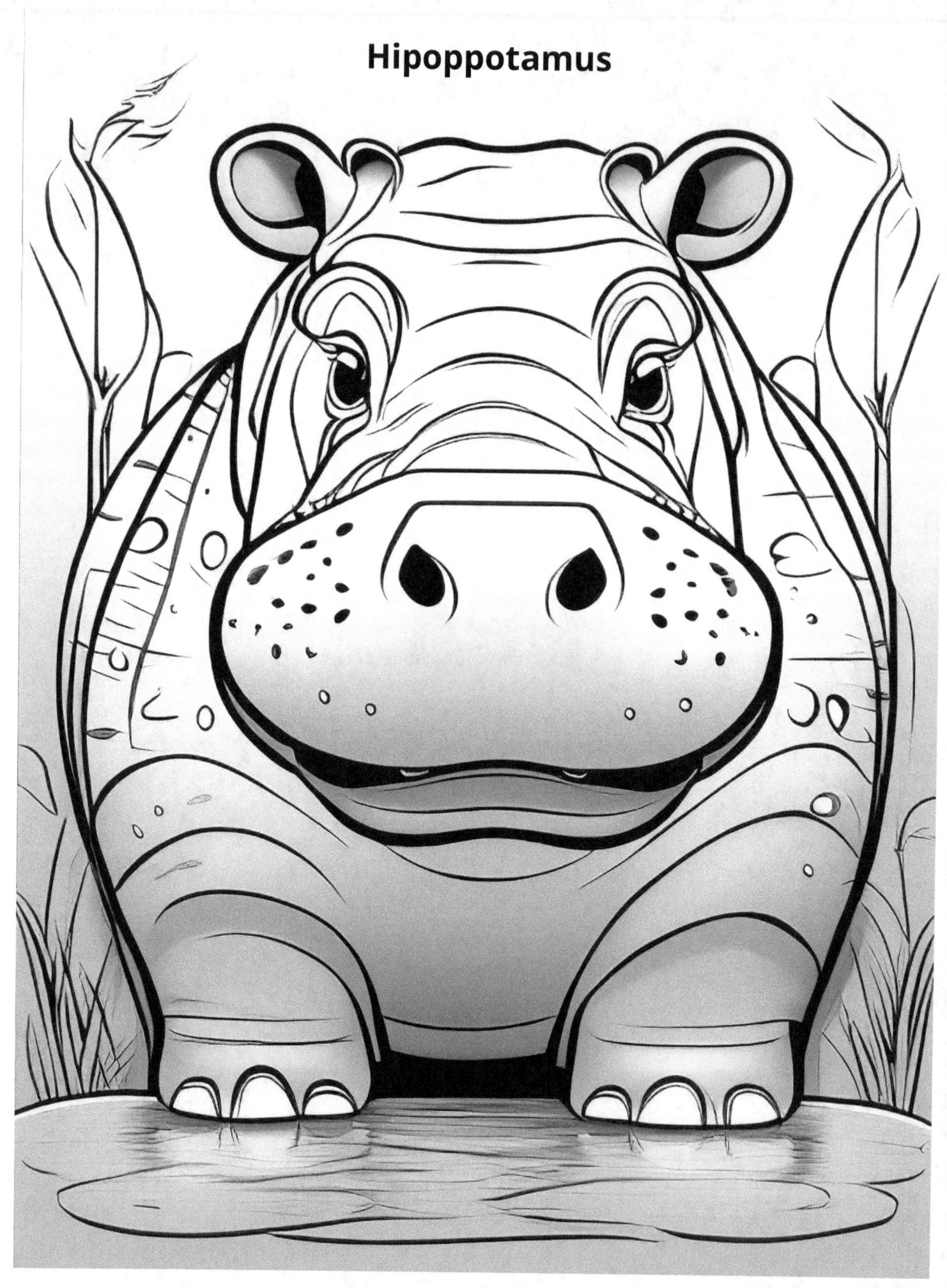

Dragon-fly

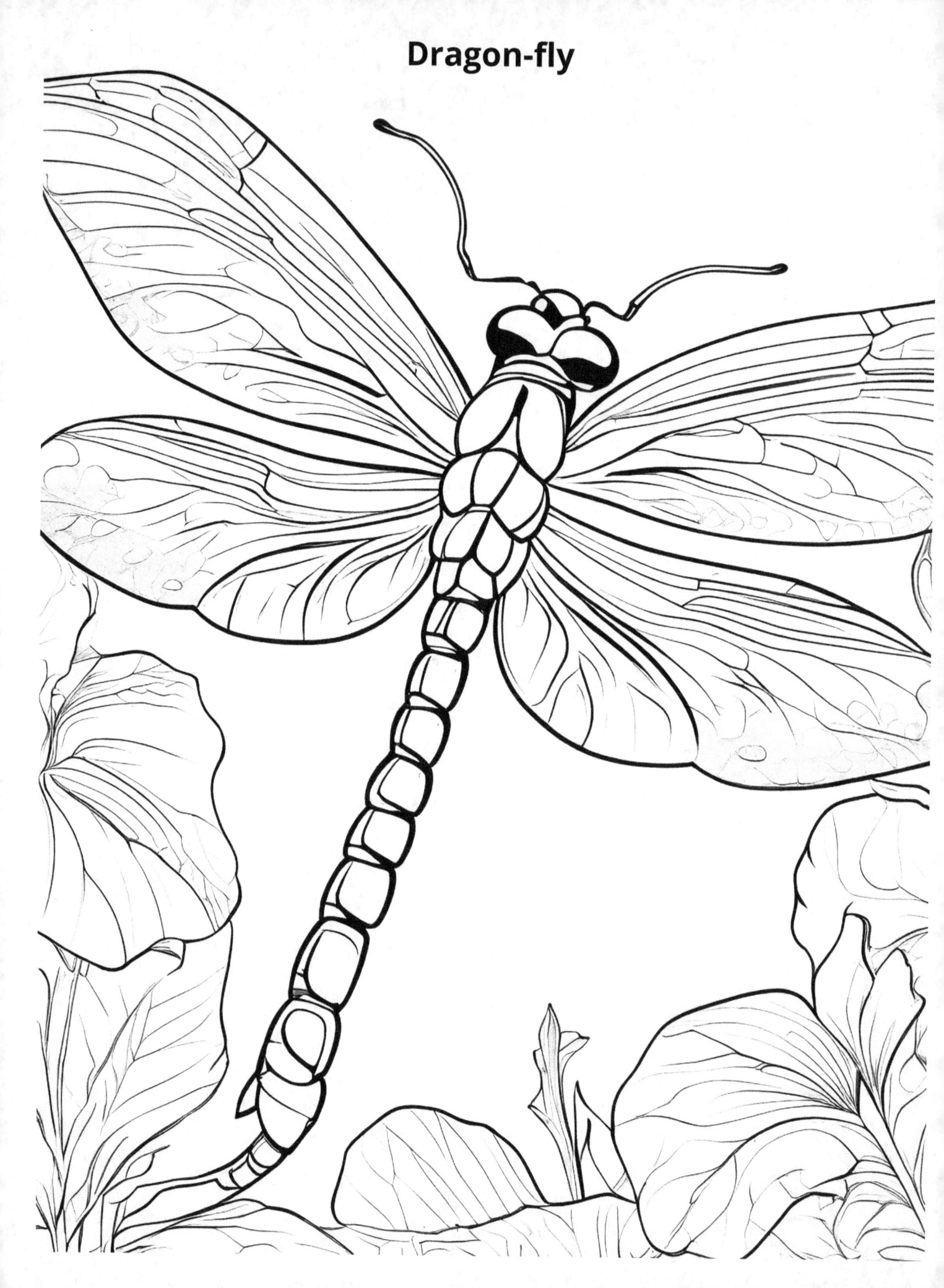

Frog

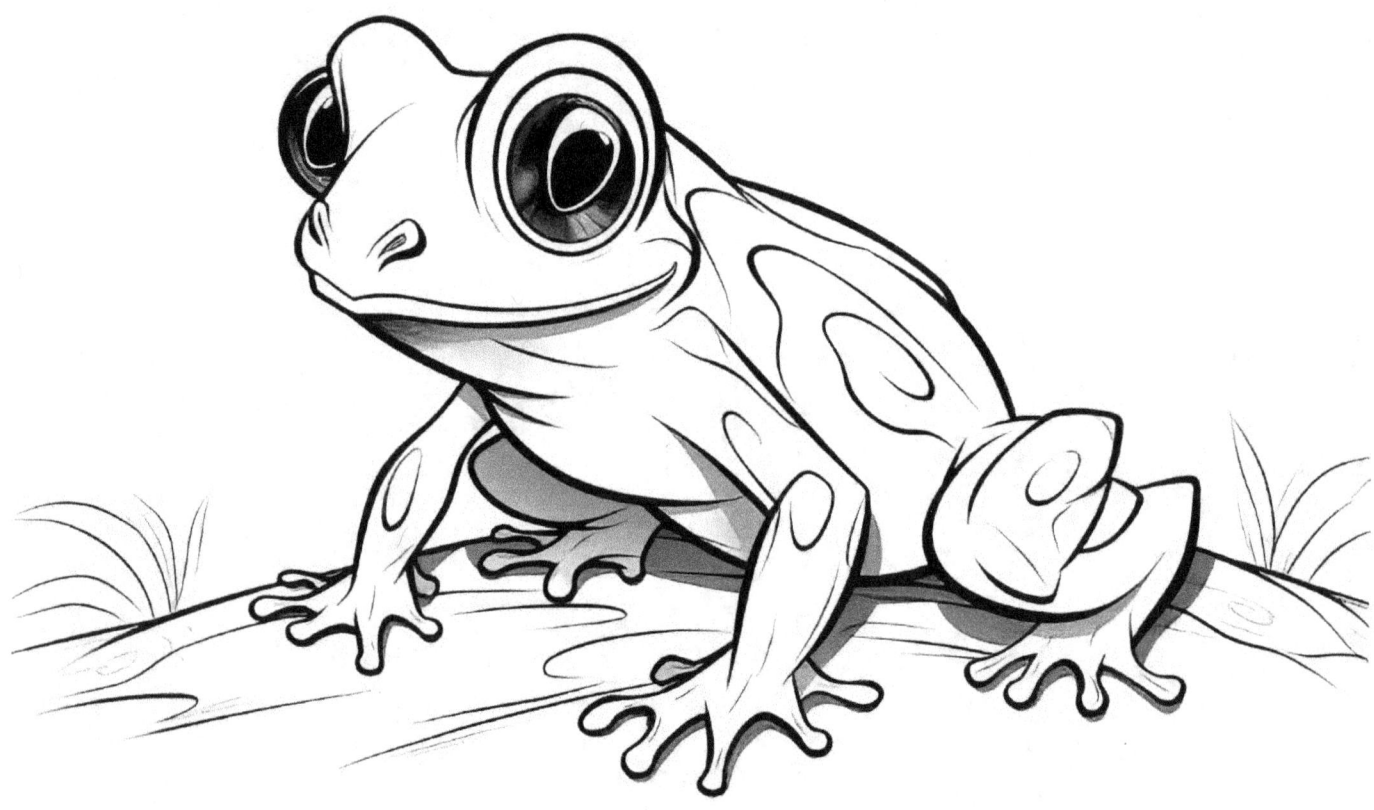

Rhino

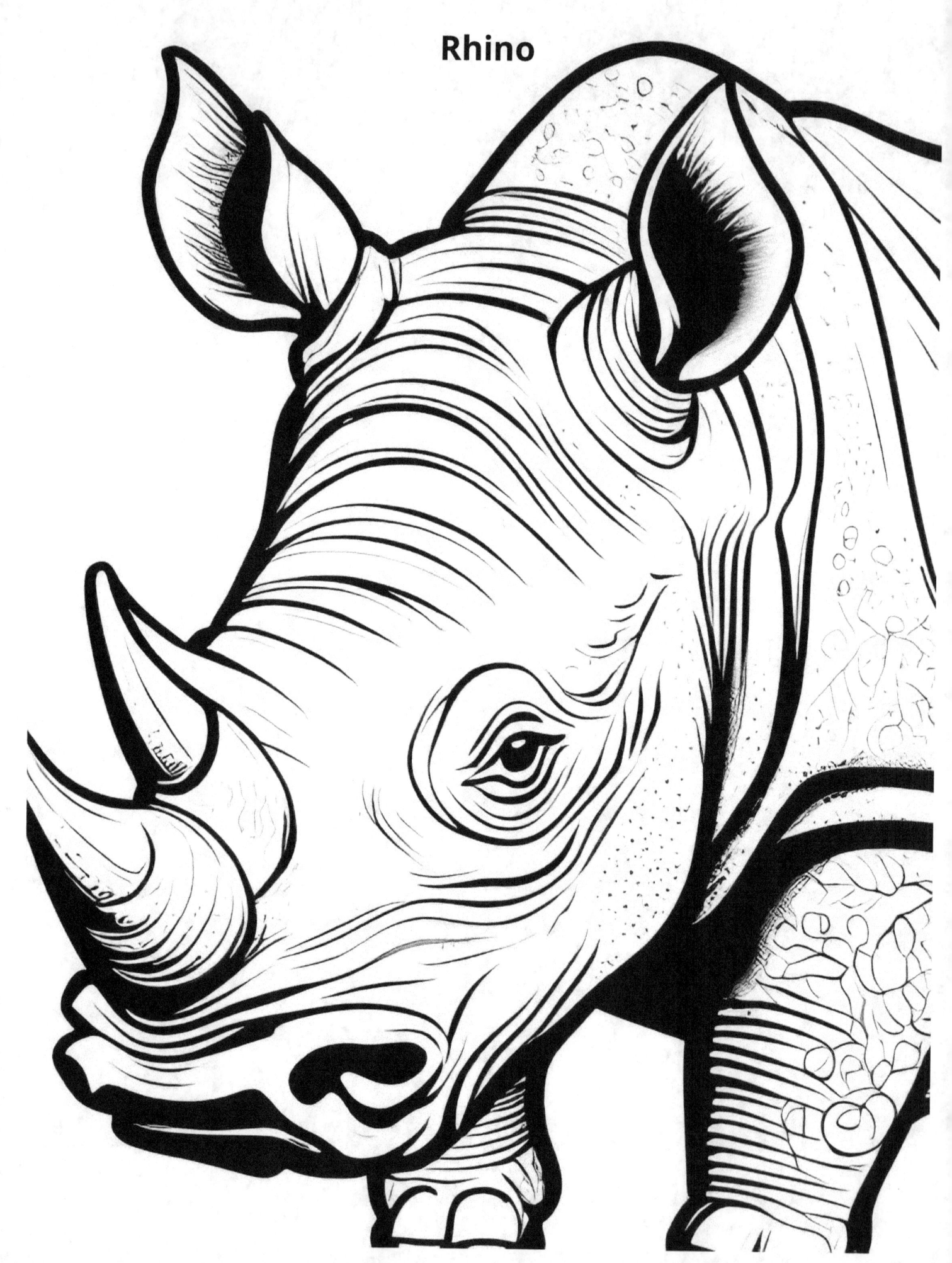

Otter

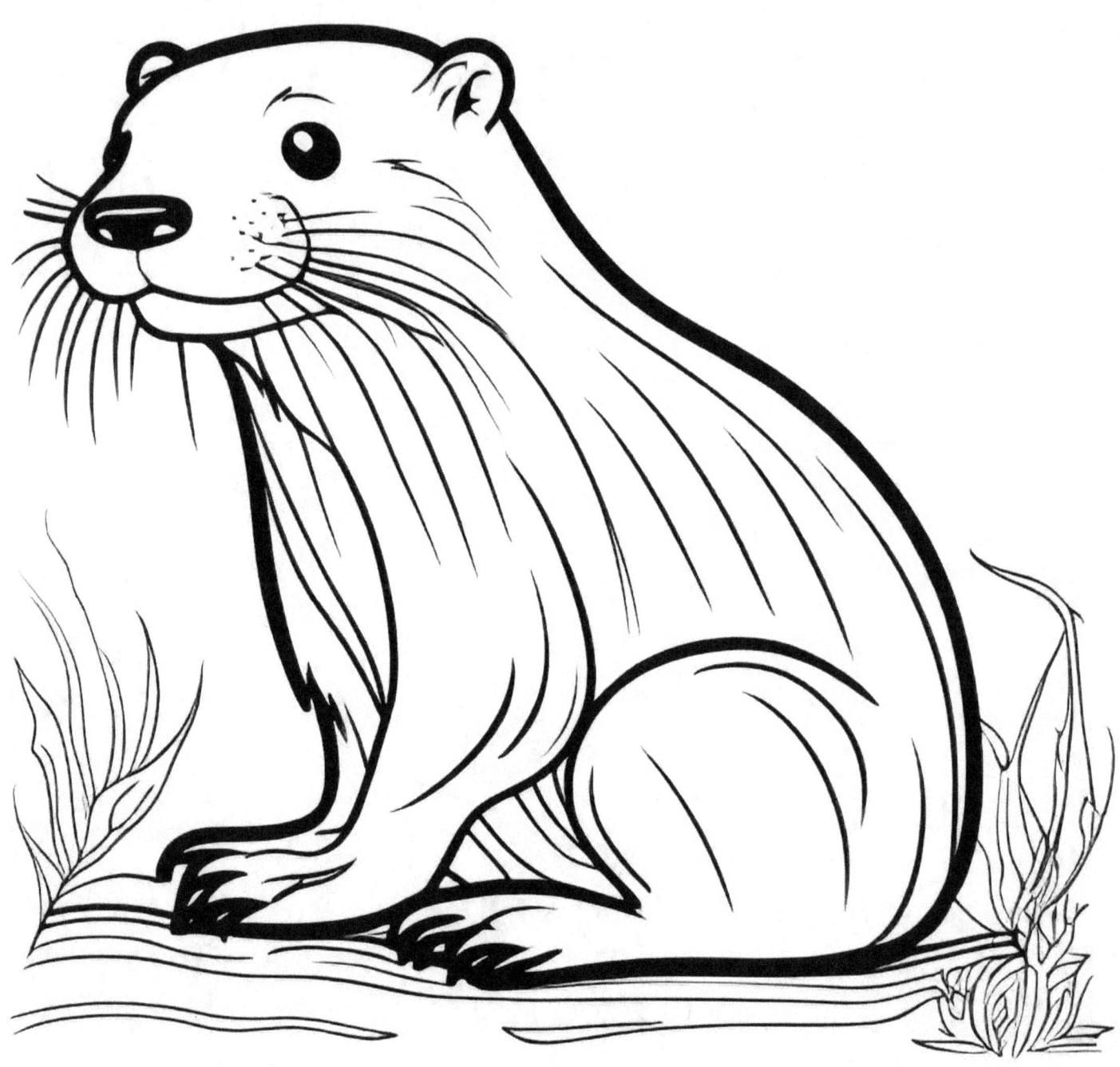

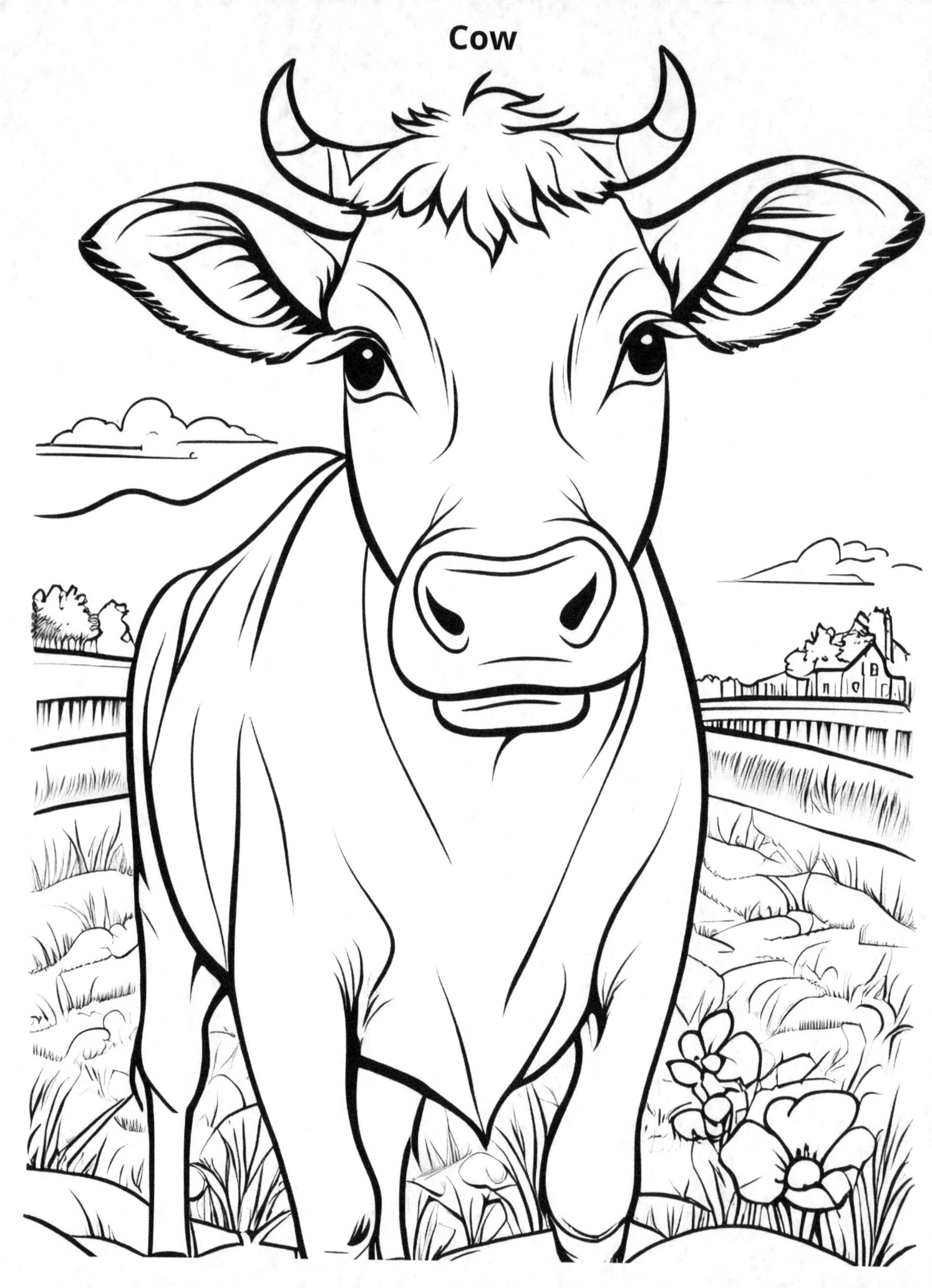

Cow

Lemur

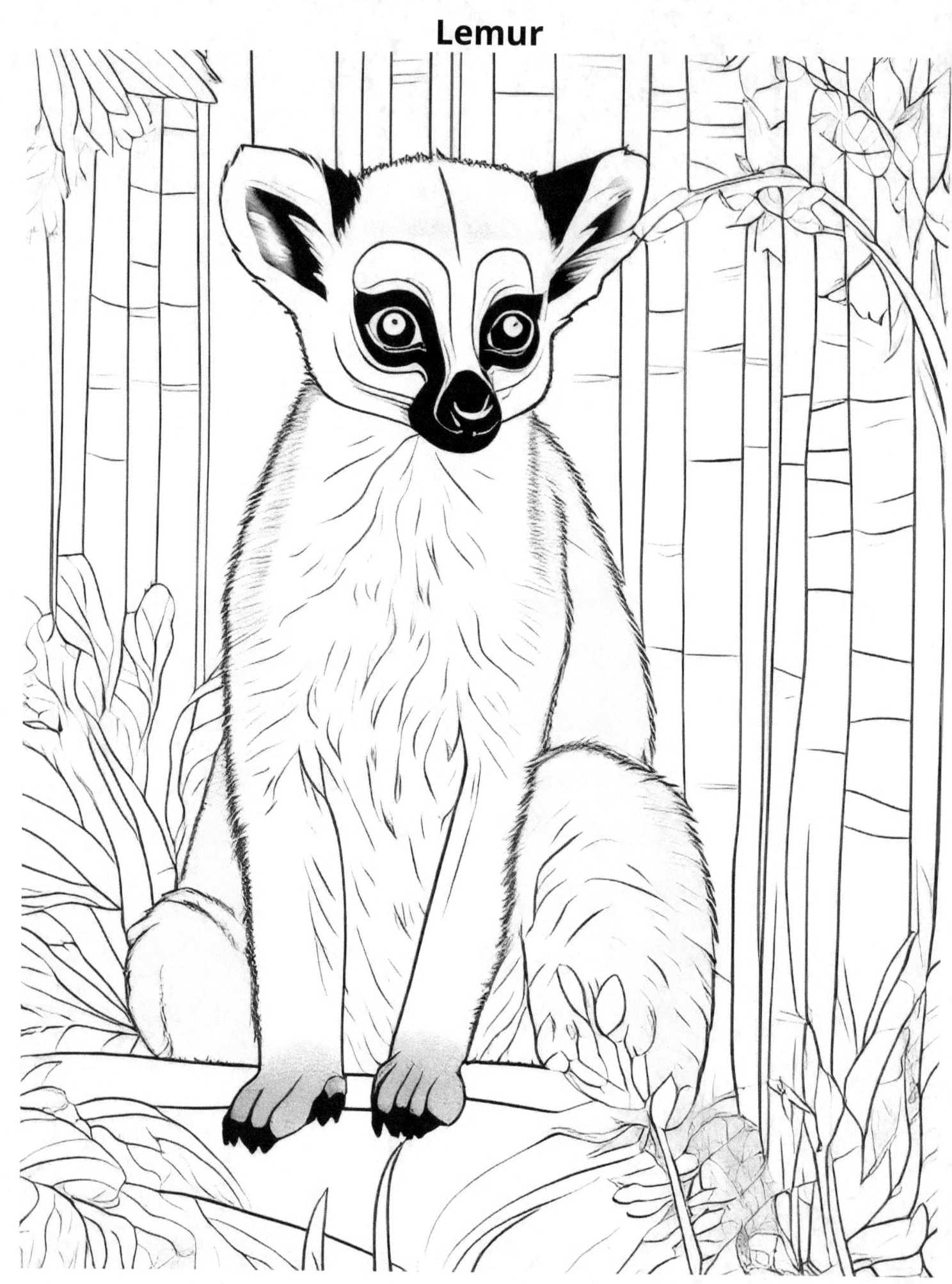

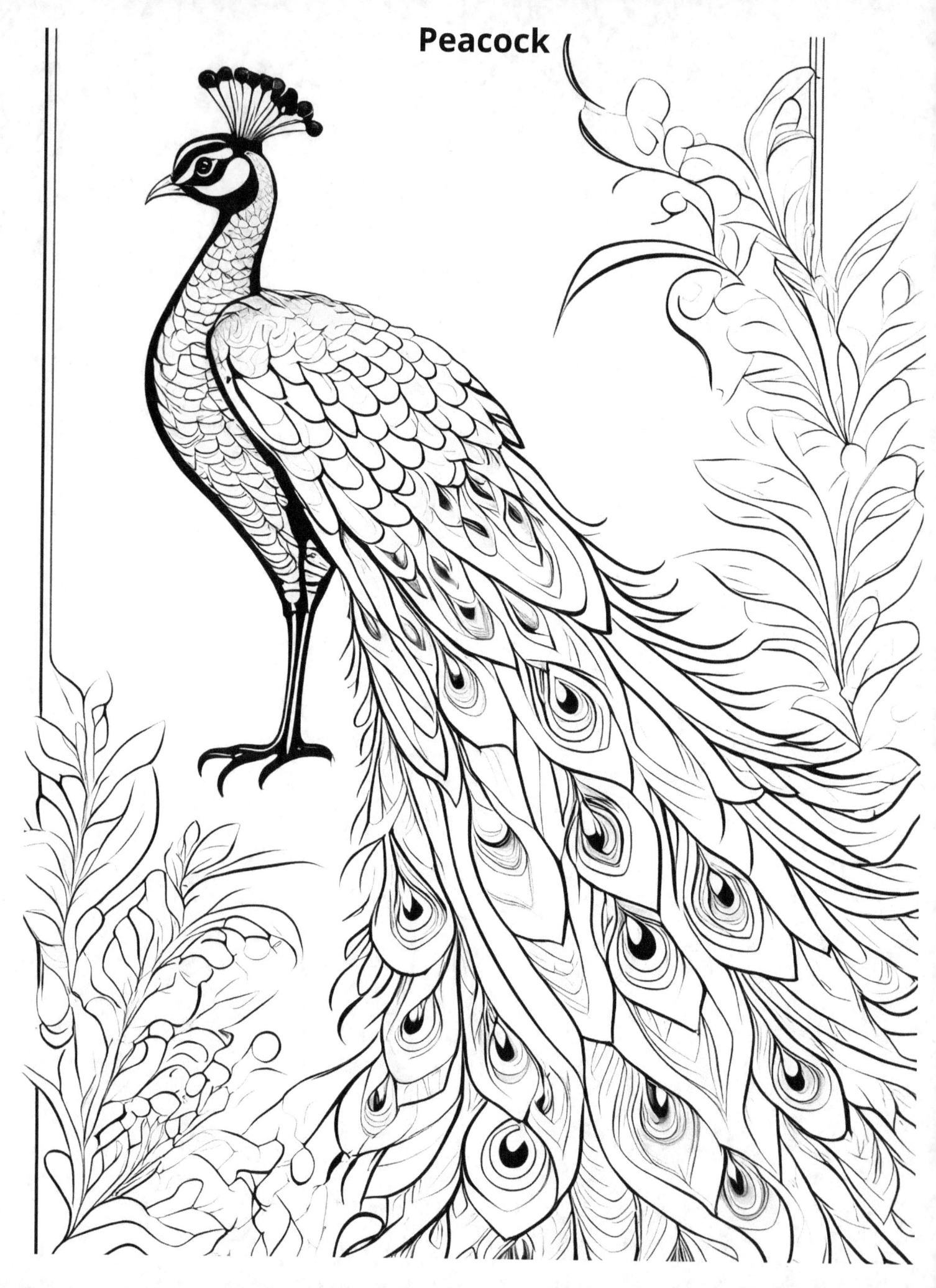

Peacock

Mandarin Duck

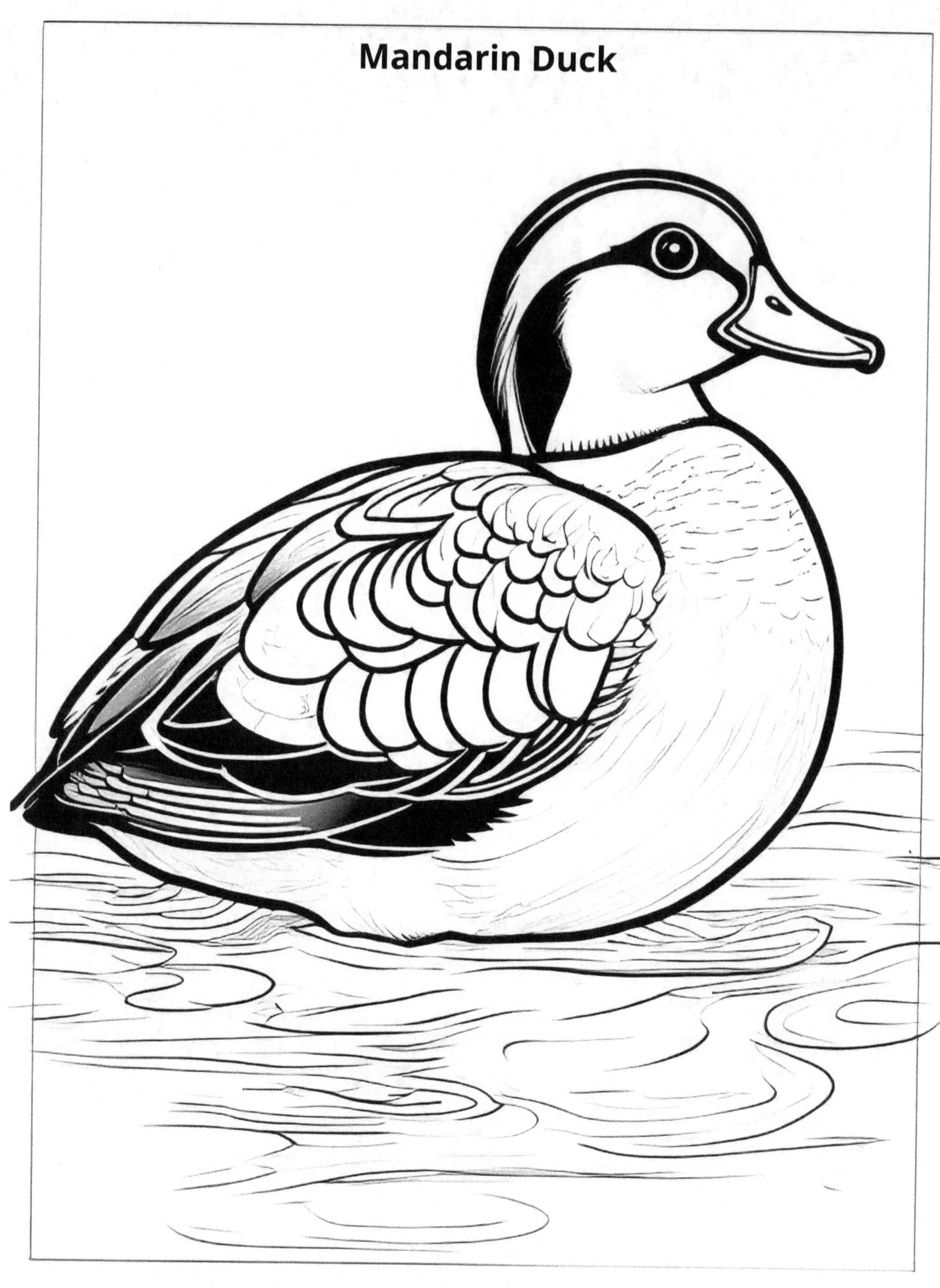

Toucan

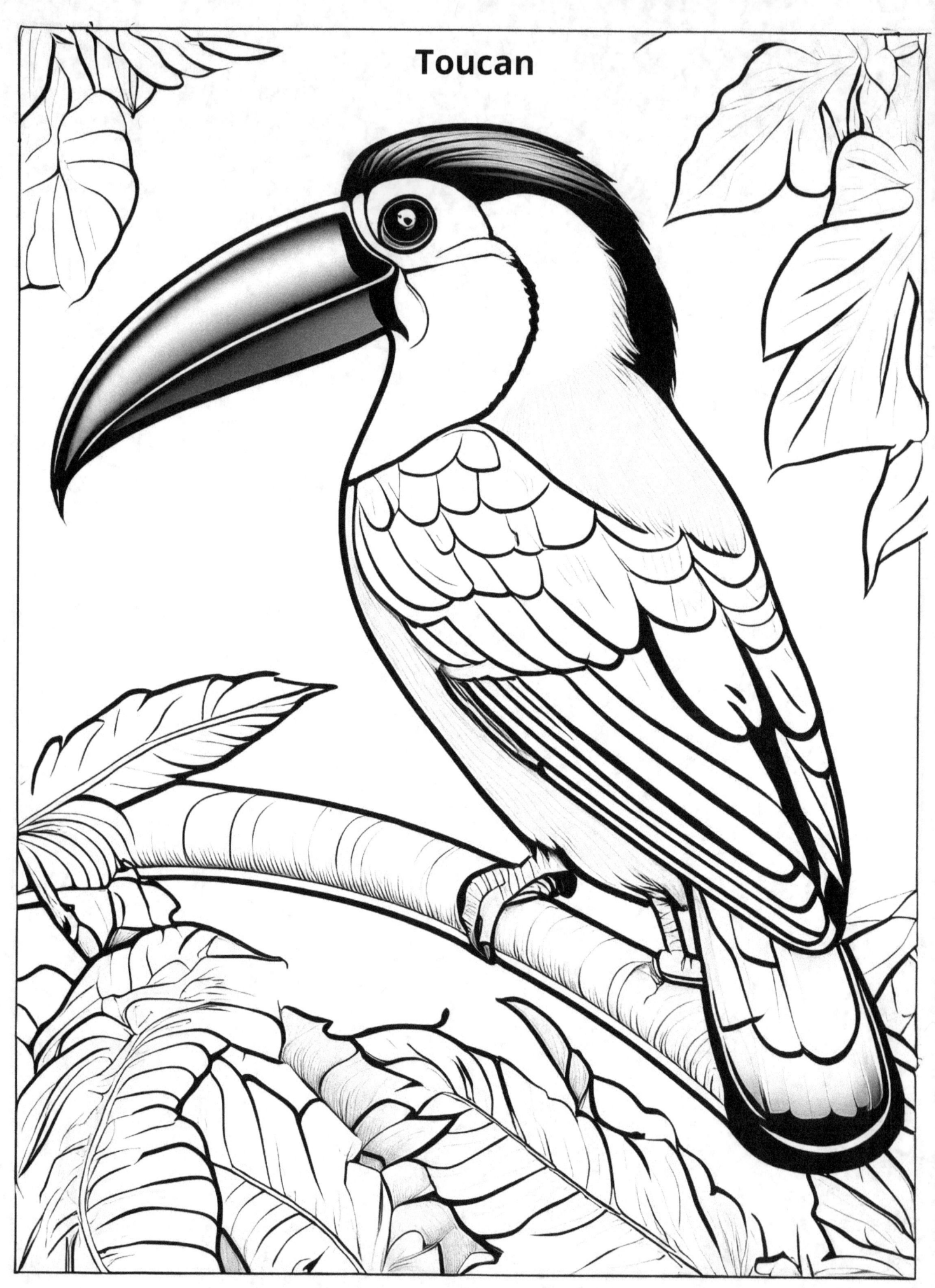

Penguin

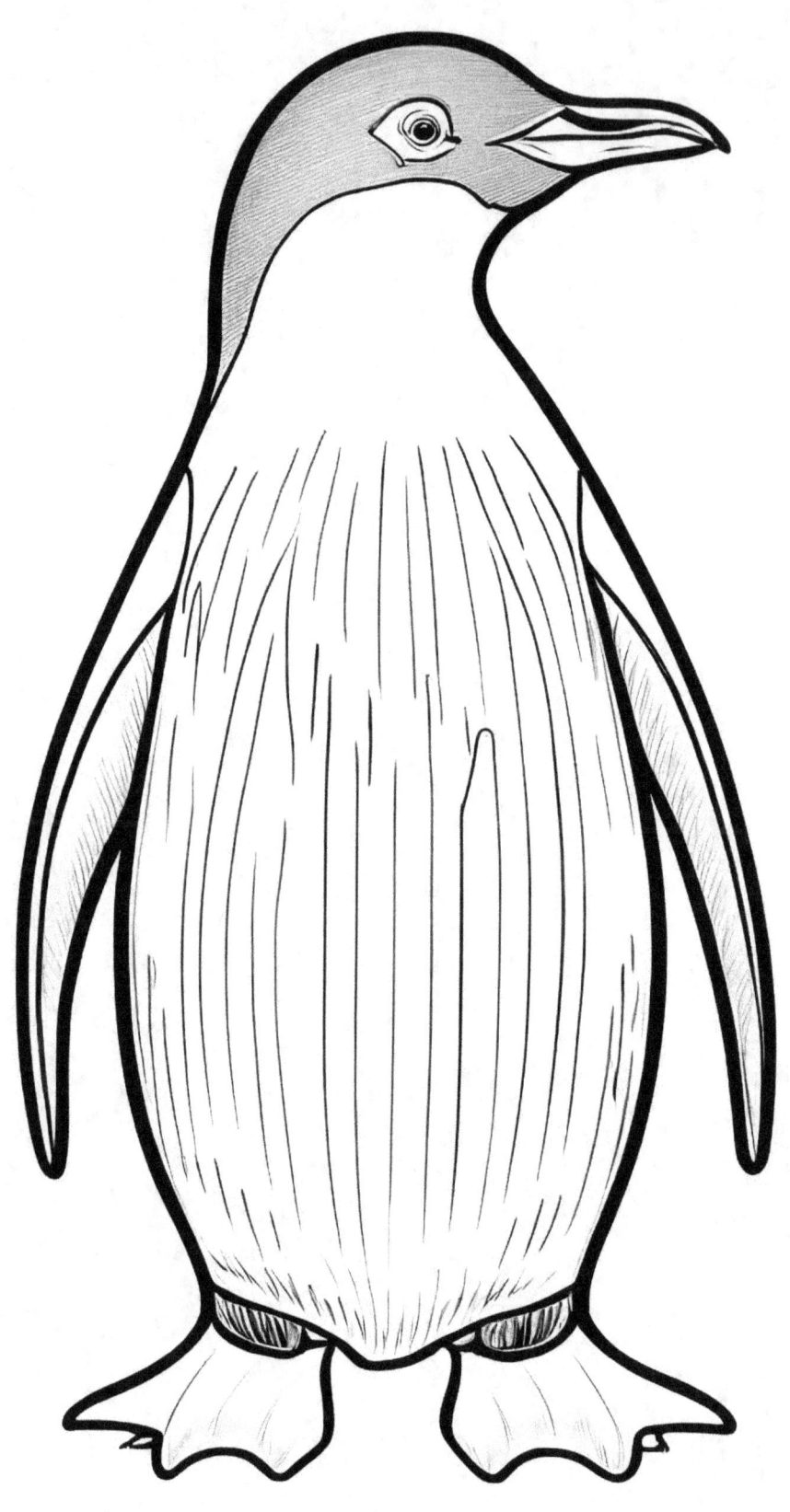

Butterfly

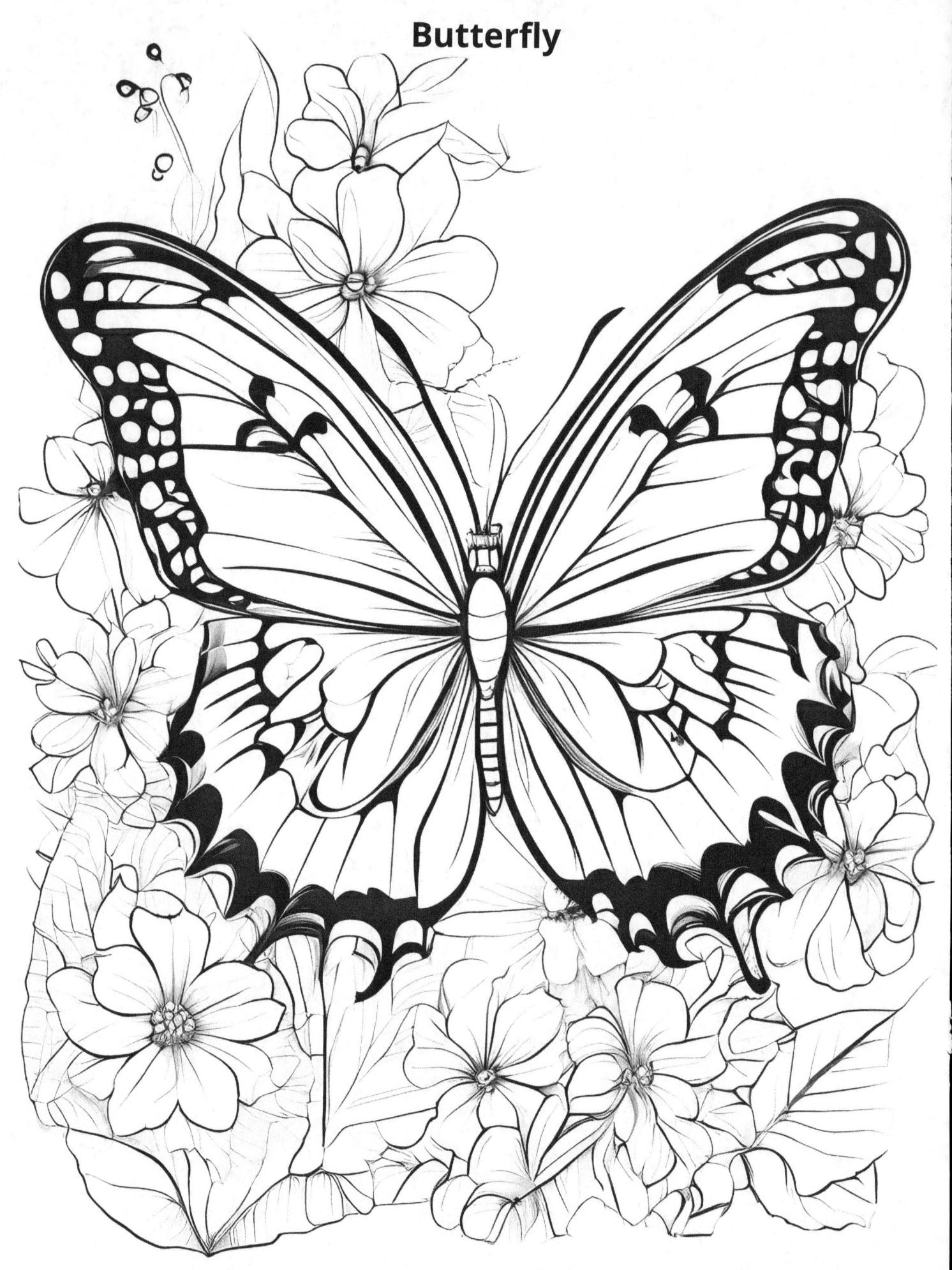

Camel

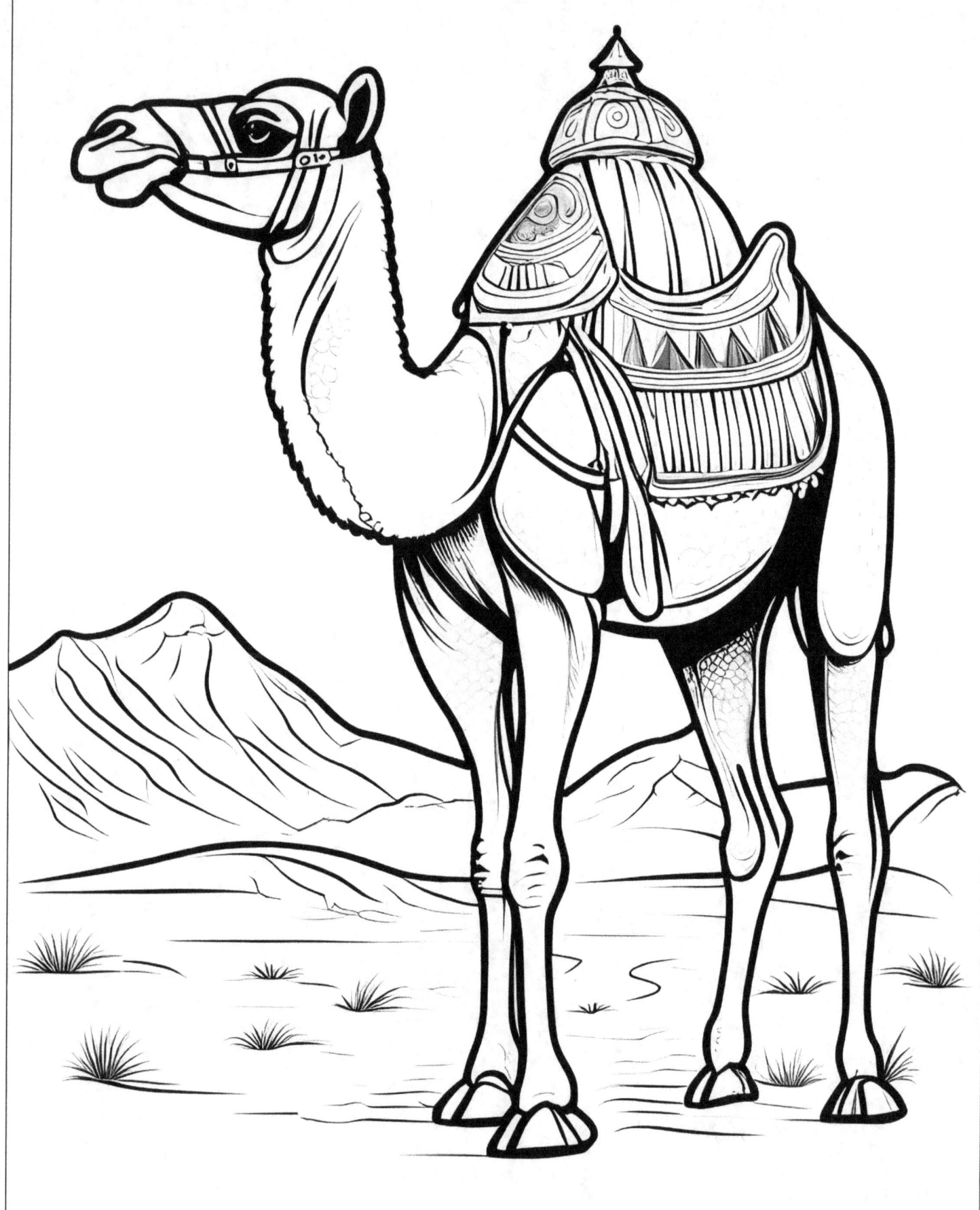

Jaburu

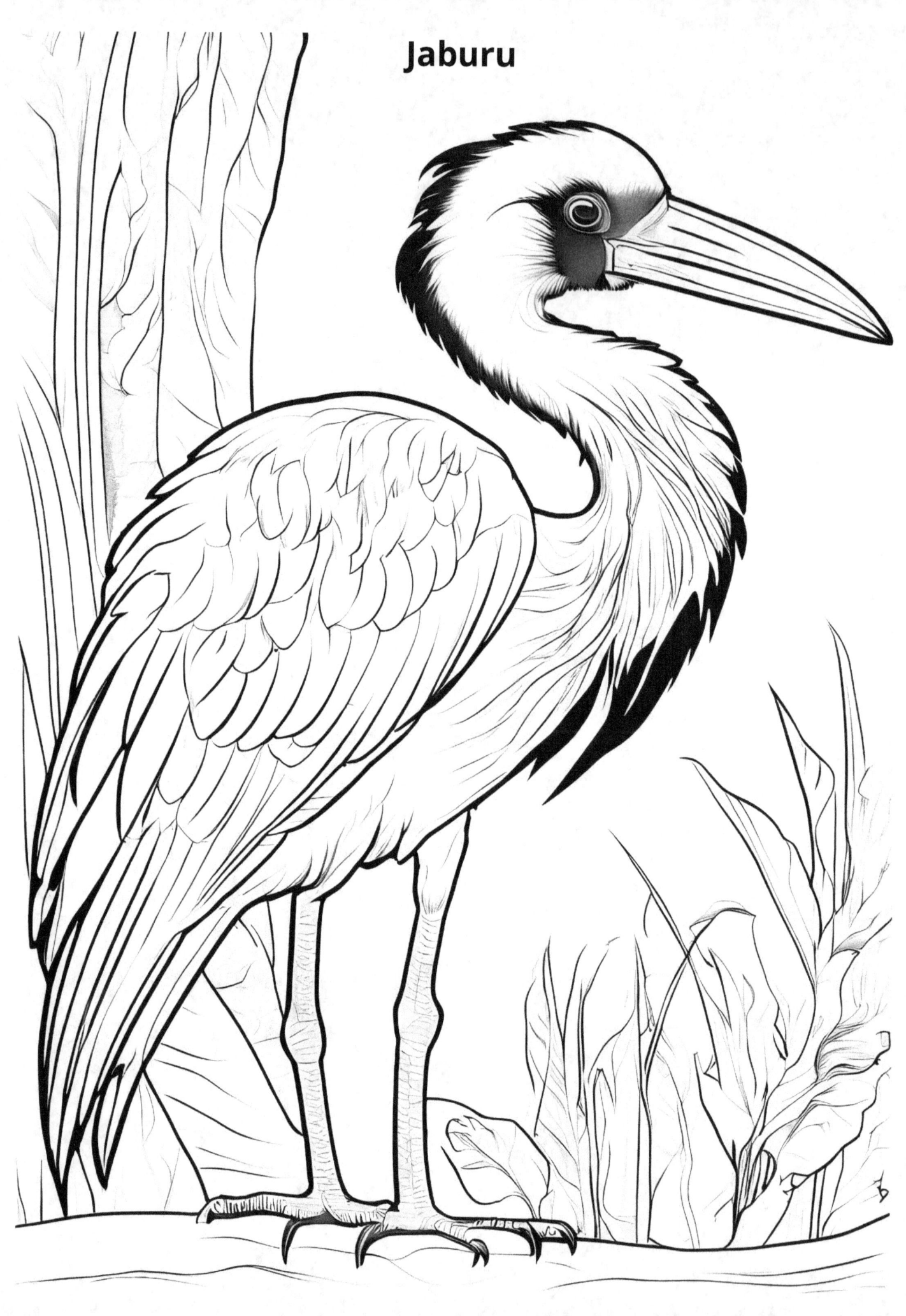

Chameleon

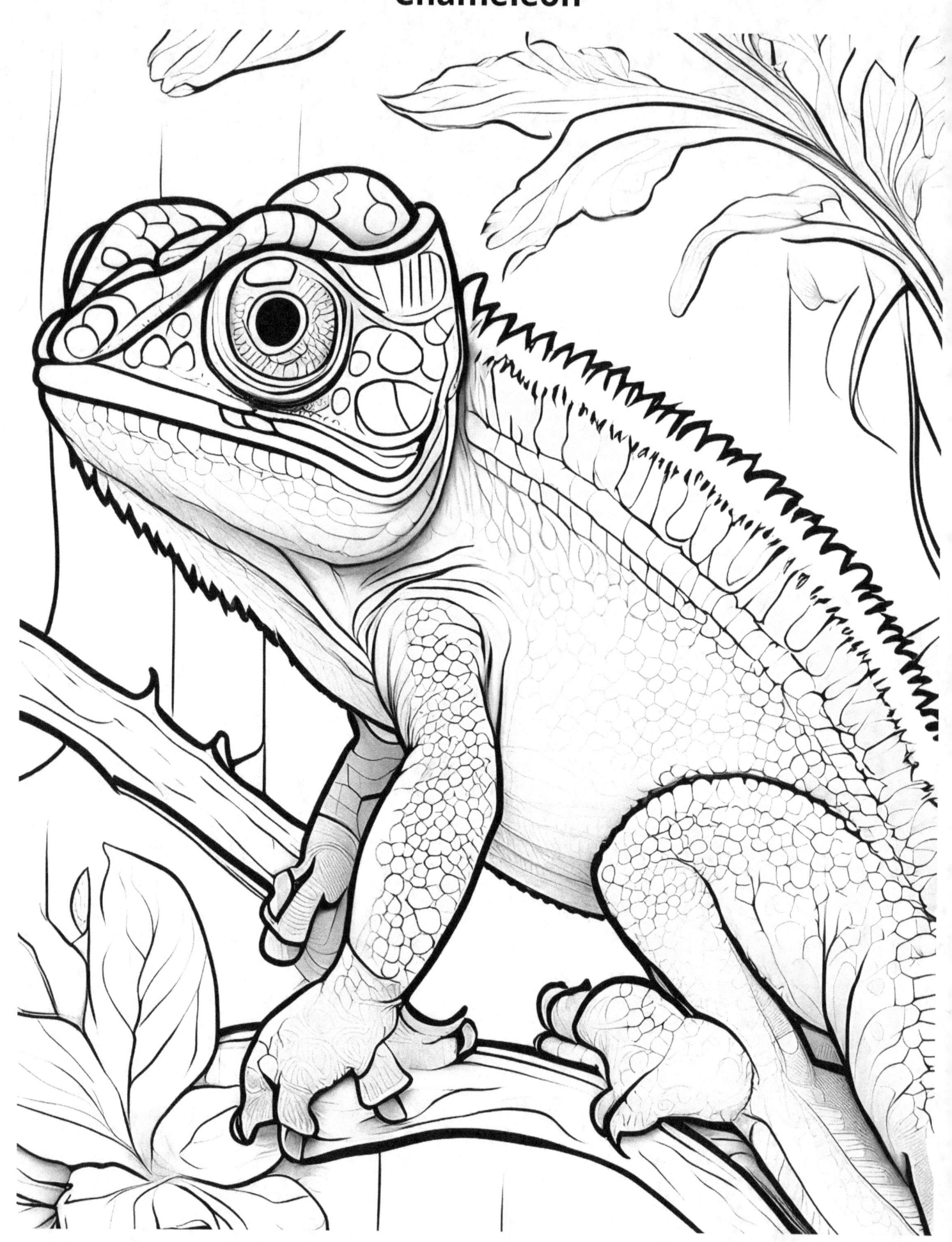

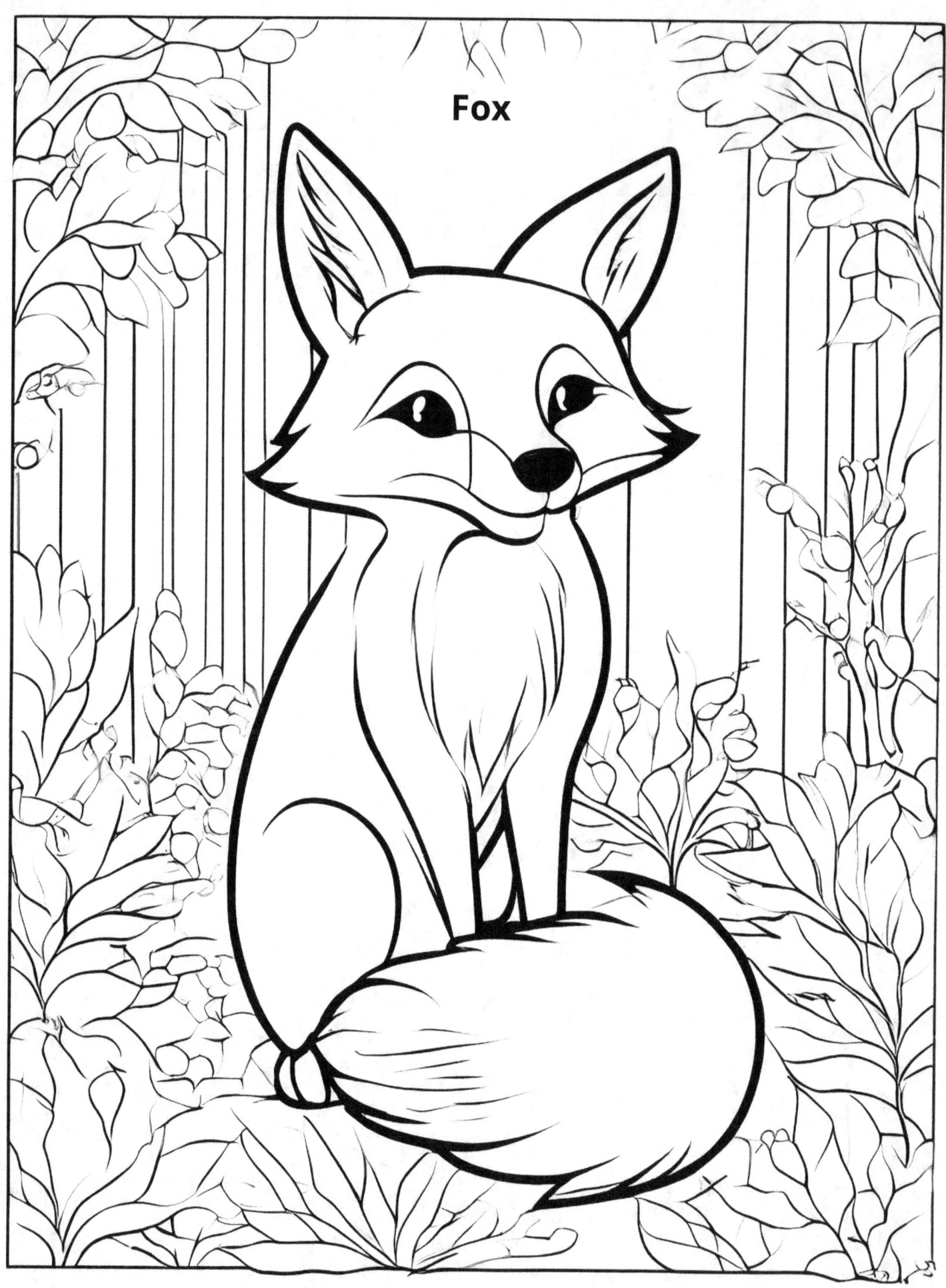

Fox

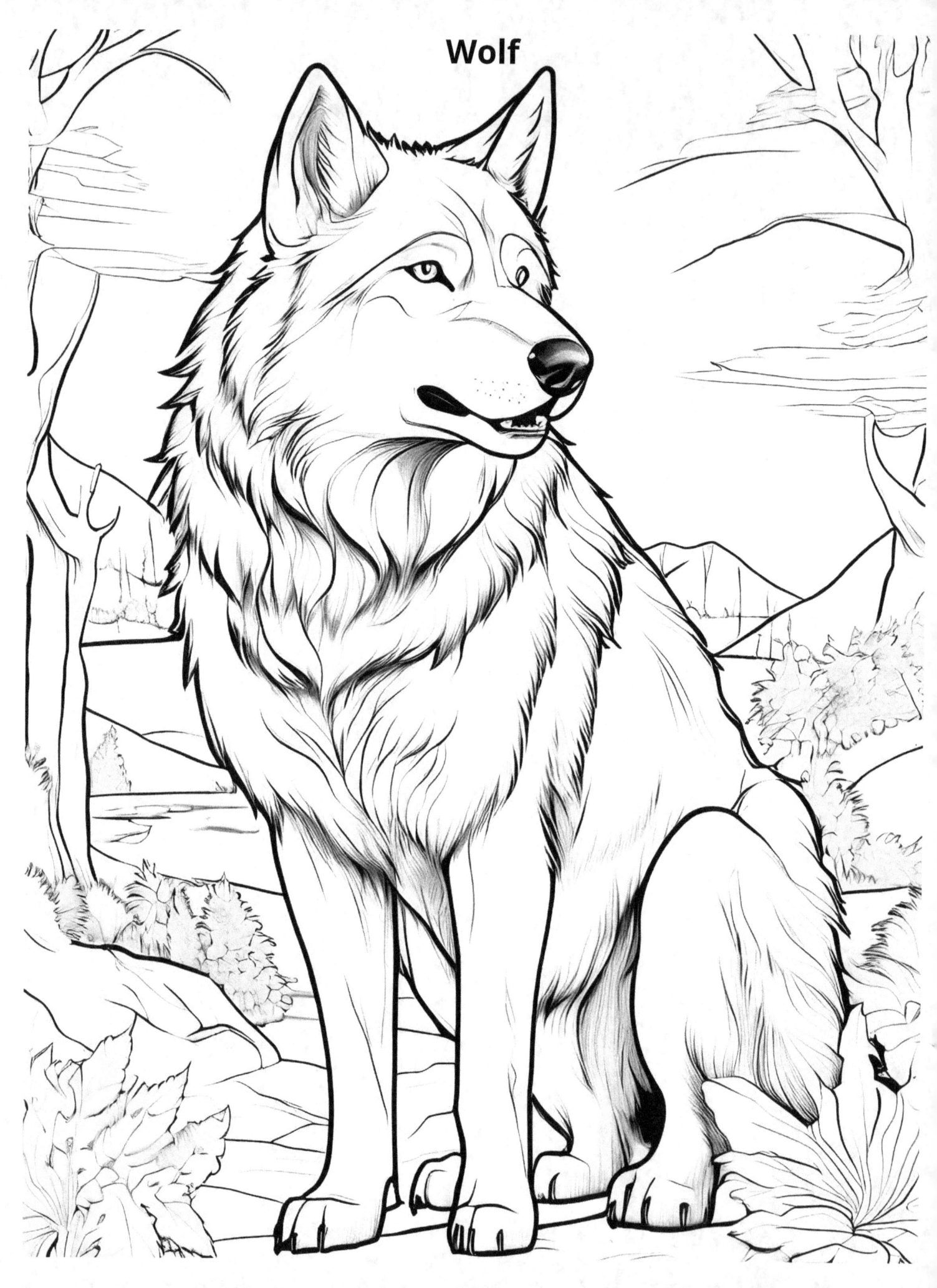

Sea Turtle

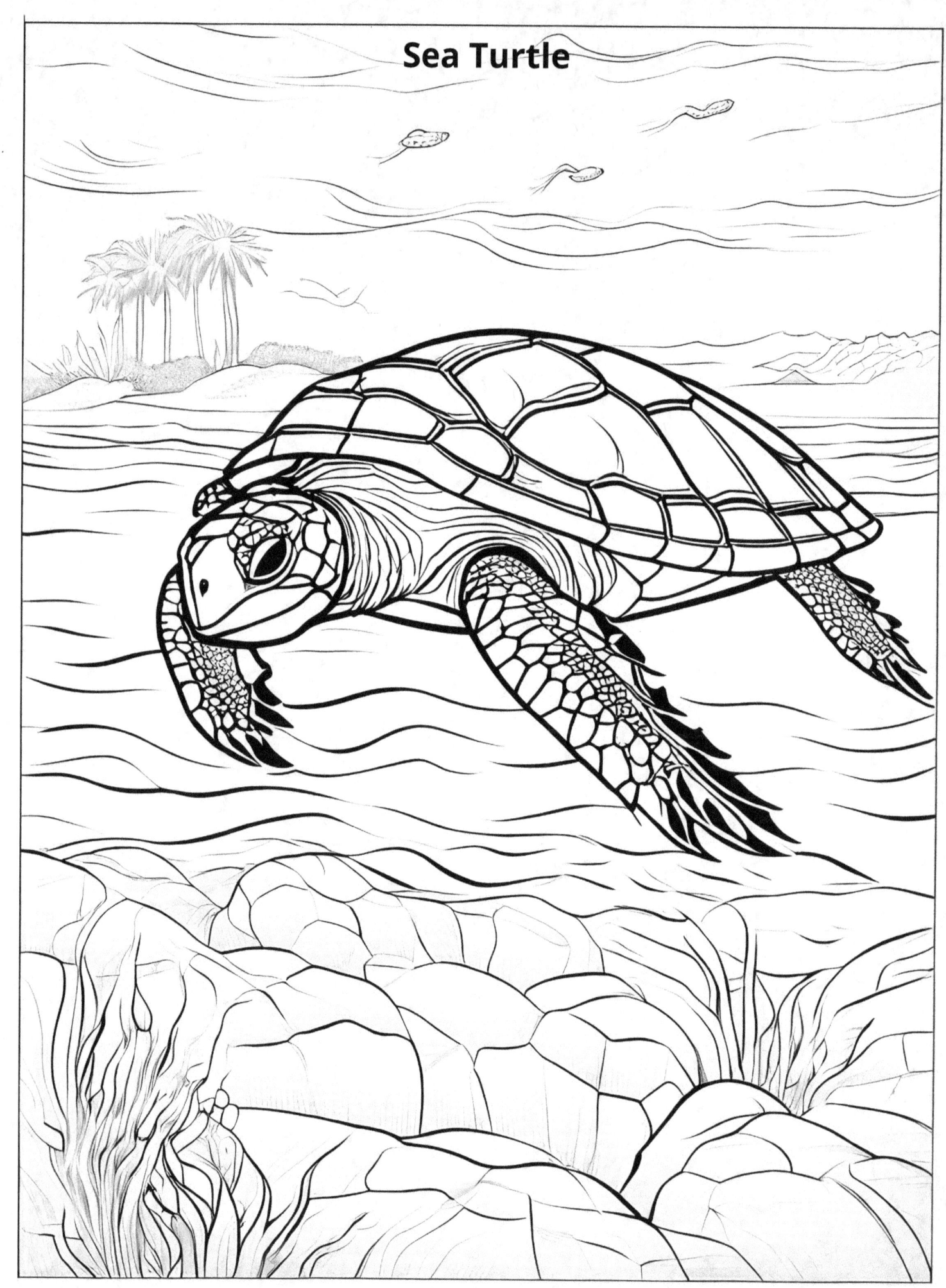

Jabuti-Tinga

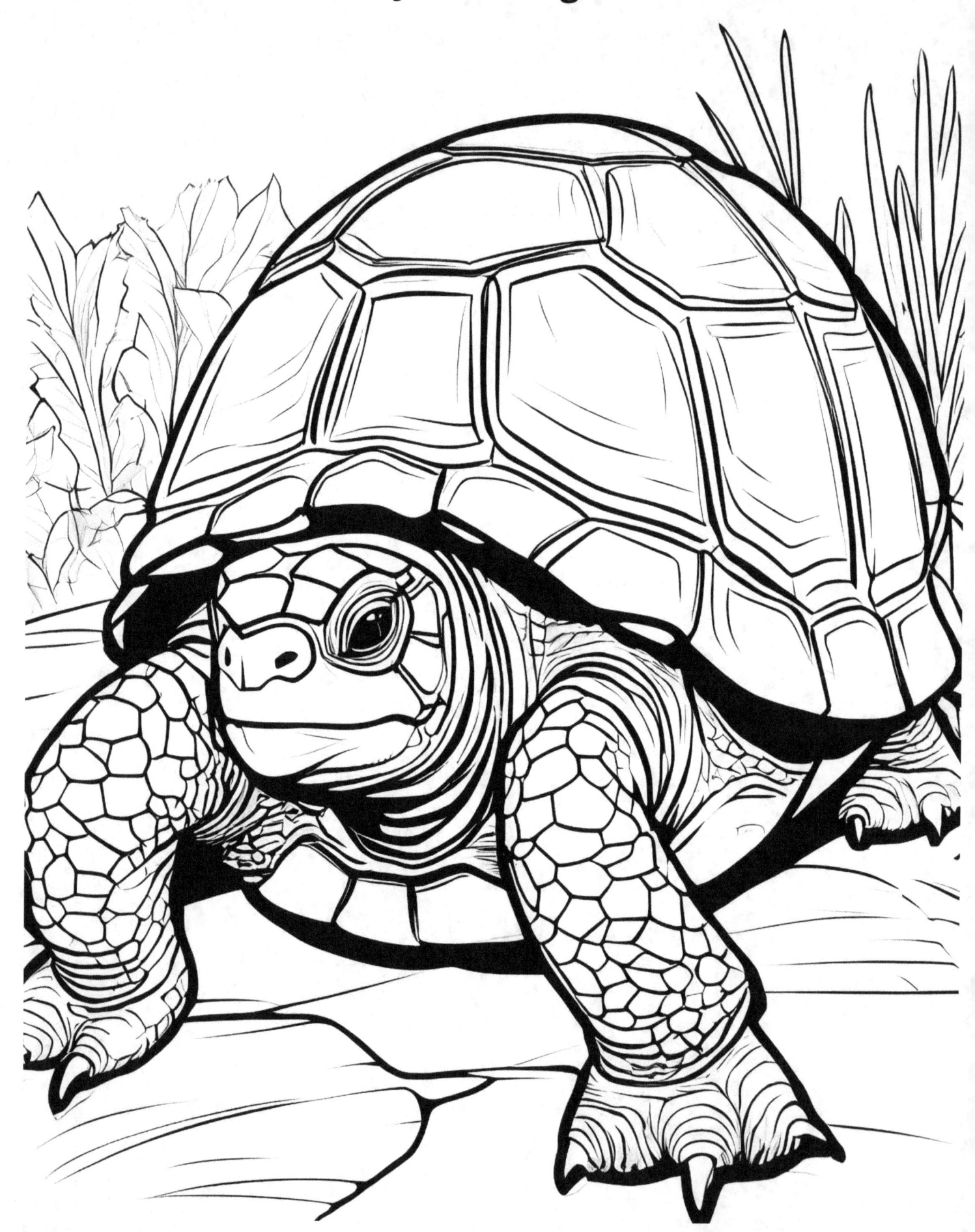

www.ingramcontent.com/pod-product-compliance
Lightning Source LLC
Chambersburg PA
CBHW080959290526

45795CB00009B/3005

* 9 7 9 8 8 7 9 3 4 3 4 5 8 *